Roles, Rights, and Responsibilities in UK Education

Roles, Rights, and Responsibilities in UK Education

Tensions and Inequalities

Hilary McQueen

ROLES, RIGHTS, AND RESPONSIBILITIES IN UK EDUCATION
Copyright © Hilary McQueen, 2014.

Softcover reprint of the hardcover 1st edition 2014 978-1-137-39800-0

All rights reserved.

First published in 2014 by PALGRAVE MACMILLAN® in the United States—a division of St. Martin's Press LLC, 175 Fifth Avenue, New York, NY 10010.

Where this book is distributed in the UK, Europe and the rest of the world, this is by Palgrave Macmillan, a division of Macmillan Publishers Limited, registered in England, company number 785998, of Houndmills, Basingstoke, Hampshire RG21 6XS.

Palgrave Macmillan is the global academic imprint of the above companies and has companies and representatives throughout the world.

Palgrave® and Macmillan® are registered trademarks in the United States, the United Kingdom, Europe and other countries.

ISBN 978-1-349-48522-2   ISBN 978-1-137-39024-0 (eBook)
DOI 10.1057/9781137390240

Library of Congress Cataloging-in-Publication Data

Roles, rights, and responsibilities in UK education : tensions and inequalities / edited by Hilary McQueen.
    pages cm
   Includes bibliographical references and index.

 1. Education—Great Britain. 2. Education—Aims and objectives—Great Britain. 3. Education and state—Great Britain. 4. Right to education—Great Britain. 5. Education—Parent participation—Great Britain. 6. Education—Philosophy. I. McQueen, Hilary.
   LA632.R58 2014
   379.41—dc23
                                            2014024029

A catalogue record of the book is available from the British Library.

Design by Amnet.

First edition: December 2014

10 9 8 7 6 5 4 3 2 1

Contents

List of Tables		vii
Acknowledgments		ix
1	Introduction *Preface by Chris Husbands*	1
2	Governance *Preface by Meg Maguire*	17
3	Learners *Preface by John Webber*	47
4	Parents *Preface by Miriam E. David*	79
5	Teachers *Preface by Bryan Cunningham*	105
6	Tensions and Inequalities Revisited: Roles, Rights, Responsibilities and Recognition *Preface by Paddy McQueen*	133
Appendix		157
References		163
Index		193

List of Tables

5.1	Qualified teachers by gender and school type (rounded figures, in thousands)	129
A.1	State-maintained provision (publicly funded)	157
A.2	Fee-paid provision	159
A.3	Qualifications	160

Acknowledgments

I am hugely thankful to the contributors for their thoughtful additions to the chapters. Many thanks to the editorial team at Palgrave for their friendly and professional assistance.

CHAPTER 1

Introduction

> **Preface**
>
> Chris Husbands, Director and Professor of Education Policy, Institute of Education, London
>
> Around the world, governments are reforming their education systems. There is almost no education system I know of which is not in a state of rapid, often convulsive change. Across the world, education reform is increasingly seen as *the* critical policy intervention which will drive twenty-first-century economic and social success. "You have", said the OECD's Andreas Schleicher to the BBC, "two choices. You can go into the race to the bottom with China, lowering wages for low-skill jobs. Or you can try to win in innovation and competitiveness" (quoted in Coughlan, 2013). There are common themes in many reform programmes. The influential Finnish commentator Pasi Sahlberg identifies a 'global education reform movement' —GERM—characterised by standardisation, an increasing focus on literacy and numeracy, an emphasis on low-risk ways to reach learning goals, the use of corporate management models as drivers of change, and the adoption of test-based accountability (see, e.g., Sahlberg, 2011), although in practice reform programmes work themselves out in distinctive ways in different cultural and political contexts.

One of the things reform programmes do, wherever they are and however they work out, is shift not only the roles, rights and responsibilities of key actors in education—parents and carers, school principals and teachers, governments and policy makers, learners and students—but also assumptions about rights and responsibilities. Policies which emphasise the importance of parental choice, for example, bring assumptions about the sorts of behaviours and engagements with education which 'good' parents are expected to demonstrate. In South Korea, four-fifths of parents pay for private tuition for their children. There are striking figures from the United States; in the early 1970s, the 20 per cent of parents with the highest incomes spent $2,700 more each year on goods and services aimed at enriching the experiences of their children (at 2008 prices) than bottom-quintile-income parents. By 2006, the corresponding inflation-adjusted difference in enrichment spending was $7,500, spent on activities such as music lessons, travel and summer camps, which could explain the differences in knowledge that are predictors of reading skills in middle and high school learners (Duncan and Murnane, 2011).

As the discussions in this book demonstrate, questions about roles, rights and responsibilities in education are both contested and far from new. Every assertion of a right—for example, school or teacher autonomy, parental choice or government initiative—involves a claim not only about authority but also about, potentially, trespass on the autonomy of others; it turns out that education is a crowded territory in which different actors trip over each other or bump into each other as they try to discharge their roles. It calls to mind Gore Vidal's famously acid assertion that 'it is not enough to succeed—others must fail'. Ideally, of course, every assertion of a right carries a corresponding responsibility, though it is not always apparent that it does. Roles are enacted against a competing swirl of claims to rights and either the discharge of or shirking from responsibilities.

We are living through extraordinarily rapid change in the relationships between rights and responsibilities, which means that roles are changing commensurately fast. Education, of course, is both a public good—the process by which any society socialises the next generation—and a positional good—the means by which some individuals acquire the means to succeed. For a century and a half, the assumption has been that because education is a public good, it should be publicly funded, and that the provision of education—the provision of schooling, of the infrastructure for higher education, of teacher education—is a core responsibility of government. Just as governments increase their expectations of the outcomes of education and drive their education systems ever harder, so they are looking for more diverse sources of funding. Education markets are developing rapidly, shifting yet again assumptions about rights and responsibilities. This book explores questions of rights and responsibilities and of the roles education actors assume in different education settings, under different assumptions and at times of rapid change. The chapters that follow are a reminder of just how complex and fascinating the relationships between rights, responsibilities and roles are.

Why This Book?

I have been learning, teaching, or doing both at the same time for as long as I can remember—so more than 50 years. Some of that time was spent in less formal teaching and learning, either as a parent or in jobs that were not directly related to education. The vast majority was spent studying or helping others to learn. Through teaching, tutoring and researching in schools, colleges and universities, I have sought, unintentionally absorbed and questioned information about the education system and its effect on individuals and society. What I value about education has come to the fore and equally has been challenged.

One example that added to a train of thought that eventually led to this book was the demand by some of my colleagues in different institutions, frustrated by the apparent dependency of some of those in further and higher education, that students take more responsibility for their learning. What did colleagues mean by this? Why weren't students being responsible, if indeed they were not? What were students doing, and what did they think they should be doing? Had they always been like this, and if so, was it inherent in young people of that age or something that had been socially constructed? Further questions ensued. Do young people have the right to succeed? If so, how can that be ensured, if indeed it should be? Isaiah Berlin (1969) pointed out that it is natural, and I would say necessary, to question issues of responsibility, for practical reasons or because humans are prone to reflect on such matters.

It would be understandable to assume that it is the role of the student to study and of the teacher to teach. However, that is much too simplistic given the shift from teacher-centred to more student-centred approaches and the increased accountability of teachers for student success. I have come across examples of extreme support. For instance, on the final day for submission, I witnessed a teacher typing a piece of coursework and offering prompts while a student suggested what to write (and this for a student without a recognised learning difficulty) in an attempt to avoid that student failing. Just this week I heard the tale of a teacher who was observed pasting pictures for a 17-year-old student to stick into a portfolio to prepare it for assessment because the student would not make the effort. A trainee teacher for whom I was a tutor was told to give everyone a distinction, serving the dual purpose of both the department and college appearing successful and the student gaining a better grade. What, I wondered, is the teacher's role within the market-driven, accountable workplace? What rights do teachers and students have? Has the notion of rights become confused with getting what is desired or with entitlement? Is it the case in education that there are "no rights without responsibility" (Giddens, 2001: 8)? Many questions led back to government policy and a "plethora of reforms" (Tomlinson, 2001: 1) accompanied by the rhetoric of necessary change, which continues to this day; so too do criticism and resistance. As I write this, *The Guardian* (August 11, 2013) comments on the "rise in number of [academy] teachers claiming they are under pressure to inflate grades," and *The Telegraph* has the headline "Universities reject Michael Gove's A-level plan" (August 12, 2013).

Thus a set of three Rs emerged from my musings—roles, rights and responsibilities—that make up the theme explored in this book. Each of these is identified with reference to governance, teachers, parents and learners. The tensions and inequalities that arise as a result of these Rs will be drawn out. A fourth R, recognition, is introduced in the concluding chapter, which offers a philosophical perspective on the tensions and inequalities argued to be bound up with the possibilities and demands for institutional, social and individual recognition that continue to dominate education systems in the United Kingdom.

The first aim of the book is to provide an overview of the educational system in the United Kingdom and some of the variation within it. A second aim is to consider the contributions made by different people in the system, including the learners themselves. A third aim of the book is to provide an overview of a system that, in spite of political rhetoric, changes in policy and reams of research, continues to a large extent to produce and reproduce social inequalities. A final aim is to indicate some of the tensions that are an inevitable part of any system which vary in the degree of impetus for change or the harm that they cause to individuals, communities and society. Whilst some suggestions are made for how to address these, it is hoped that the book will provoke readers to ponder the state of affairs and consider their own solutions.

Setting the Scene

The book's title refers to the United Kingdom, to education, and to tensions and inequalities. Regarding the United Kingdom, I will briefly outline its constituent parts and some similarities and differences in the education system of each region. I am using the term *education* here rather loosely, with the sense of all people and processes that are involved in teaching, learning and the provision of courses or qualifications. Further definition is offered later in this chapter. Regarding tensions and inequalities, a number of disagreements, conflicts, struggles and debates will become evident. This book is not arguing for one solution; rather it aims to review the state of affairs from different perspectives, specifically governance, educators and those in associated services, parents and learners. The theme is broad, particularly as each stage of the education system is referred to (pre-school, primary, secondary, further and higher education) as well as different parts of the United Kingdom. There is an inevitable trade-off between breadth and depth, although reference to further reading will be included throughout, and the contributions from expert colleagues will add depth to the discussion.

The United Kingdom and Education

Before embarking on the main themes of this book, it might be helpful to define the United Kingdom. I first came across the Scottish education system when I left what I assumed unthinkingly was the usual, British (English) system and travelled more than 500 miles to attend Edinburgh University. There I found, to my great surprise, that many of my contemporaries from Scotland were a year younger than me and had studied Highers, not A-levels (see the appendix for an overview of qualifications). In addition, for some time I was ignorant of the fact that a three-year honours degree in England took four years in Scotland and that the fourth year depended on selection to continue. It may well be that you are reading this book without complete knowledge of the British system and perhaps share similar naïve assumptions. In that case, it is hoped that the following discussion will make the situation clearer.

Great Britain is a big island that is made up of Scotland, England and Wales. The United Kingdom, sometimes confusingly referred to as Britain, politically consists of Northern Ireland, Wales, England and Scotland (Burns, 2010). The island of Ireland (Eire in Irish) is divided into the smaller Northern Ireland, which is part of the United Kingdom, and the larger Republic of Ireland, which is not. The Republic of Ireland is politically separate and therefore will not be included in the chapters that follow. Each part of the United Kingdom shares features of the education system, yet there are some important differences (see, e.g., Phillips, 2000, and Gearon, 2002, for more detailed descriptions and analyses of similarities and differences). One difference is that Northern Ireland and some regions of England (particularly the southeast region and Lincolnshire) have retained grammar schools as part of maintained (state) education, although pupils are no longer routinely tested for entrance. Tables have been included in the appendix to give an overview of the differences in structure and qualifications within the United Kingdom.

The fact that there are different systems within a larger, currently interdependent one is in itself a source of tension and inequality. 'Which system is better?' one might ask, and this is usually tested by finding out which system leads to greater exam success. Disagreement about the purpose and structure of education is partly founded on the demand by Scotland, Wales and Northern Ireland to be recognised as independent nations within the United Kingdom that have to contend with different social and economic needs; thus the constituent parts of the United Kingdom are distinguished educationally to some degree by what young people should learn about and therefore by the curriculum. For example, the following assertions are peculiar to the school curriculum for Wales, which includes the national curriculum (Welsh Government, 2007):

- [It] supports government policy, including: bilingualism, Curriculum Cymreig/Wales, Europe and the World, equal opportunities, food and fitness, sustainable development and global citizenship and the world of work and entrepreneurship;
- [It] continues to deliver a distinctive curriculum that is appropriate for Wales.

The national curriculum (for England and Wales) was implemented in 1988 and is outlined in the Education Act (2002). It is currently under review. Northern Ireland devised its own curriculum, which shares features with the English and Welsh versions but includes personal development and mutual understanding up to key stage one (so between the ages of three and seven) as well as the Irish language for some schools. Education for Mutual Understanding (EMU) is one strategy that Northern Ireland has adopted in an attempt to build bridges between the majority Protestant and minority Catholic populations. In Scotland, the Curriculum for Excellence for learners aged 3 to 18 is non-statutory (Education Scotland), and there are differently named qualifications compared with other parts of the United Kingdom.

Notwithstanding these and other differences, both between and within the nations of the United Kingdom, there are shared points of reference that, depending on one's perspective, indicate considerable similarity. At present, too, the countries of the United Kingdom are inextricably connected. In a report on education in a devolved Scotland, Machin et al. (2013) point out that there are many similarities between each region of the United Kingdom that constrict the possibility of true devolution. These include defence, tax and benefit policies. In September 2014 a referendum was held to decide if Scotland would become an independent country but the majority voted 'no'.

What Is Education?

Jackson (2011) wrote a book asking the philosophically expansive question of what education is. As he says, one might use a general definition that covers some aspects of what it means to educate or be educated. The word *educate* is derived from Latin (*educare* and *educere*). Both Latin roots refer to some kind of development of young people, although *educare* implies training whereas *educere* means to draw out. Most people's experience is of the training kind whereby a teacher imposes learning rather than acting as a resource for the learner. Perhaps a school such as Summerhill in Suffolk, southeast England, demonstrates drawing out more than training, based on the founder A. S. Neill's belief that "the function of the child is to live his own life—not the life that his anxious parents think he should live, nor a life according to the purpose of the educator who thinks he knows best" ("Summerhill: The Early Days", 2004). One could add to that 'nor a life according to the purpose of the government' since policy dictates the majority of what educators are required to do and, more indirectly, how they are required do it.

The word *education* is used so frequently that its definition can seem obvious until the question of what it means is addressed. In most texts, *education* is not defined at all, or its meaning is implicit. Some authors refer to *schooling* rather than *education*; others use the terms interchangeably. *Schooling* implies learning that takes place in a formal setting, which for some authors has more negative, socially restrictive connotations than a broader education of which the school experience might be a part; "the pupil . . . is 'schooled' to confuse teaching with learning, grade advancement with education, a diploma with competence" (Illich, 1971: 1).

Education can vary therefore in the degree of its formality and the extent to which it is intentional. Rousseau ([1762] 1979) suggested three sources of education: internal development of the body and two external influences, our experience and being taught. Butler (1915) defined education as a preparation for life, an adjustment to the group one is born into, and a way to realise one's potential, if that could be known of course. Jackson's first thought involved "a socially facilitated process of cultural transmission" (2011: 9), which fits the brief references to aspects of the UK curricula above, but he extended this upon further consideration to include morals, truth and the ability to think. Indeed, it is difficult to define education without referring to what 'it' aims to do for the individual or for society. Education, particularly schooling, can never be a neutral process.

Michael Gove, appointed Secretary of State for Education for the coalition government in 2010, defined the purpose of education in a speech to the Royal Society for the Encouragement of Arts, Manufactures and Commerce (RSA) in 2009:

> I regard education as the means by which individuals can gain access to all the other goods we value—cultural, social and economic— on their terms. I believe education allows individuals to become authors of their own life story. (Gove, 2009)

This implies that all individuals can benefit from education and that it is an instrumental rather than intrinsic good. It also implies that there is consensus on what is valued, yet others would disagree. In the introduction to *Equality and Inequality in Education Policy* (Dawtrey et al., 1995: xi), the authors say that "education emerges from many… articles as being far from a radical and liberating experience for many pupils, but rather restraining, and a means of legitimizing dominant ideologies of state and society". Ward and Eden (2009: 1) simply state that "education is politics".

The idea that education can be radical and liberating is associated with philosophical notions of teaching and learning. Elias and Merriam (1995) outline six approaches that vary in purpose: behaviourist, liberal, analytic, progressive, humanistic and radical. I have applied these to consideration of adult education elsewhere (McQueen et al., 2013). Of the six approaches, the liberal approach is perhaps the most familiar and the radical the least. Approximately 2,500 years ago, the ancient Greeks laid the foundations for what became known as liberal arts education, which had the purpose of allowing wealthy Athenians to engage in political life and debate and brought with it a particular style of teaching.

> Its receipt involves becoming acquainted with great literature as well as science, and so cannot be child-centred, since children cannot be expected to know without appropriate instruction what great literature and art is. (Conway, 2010: xxiii)

Today the term *academic education* might be used, but the potentially divisive origins that separated wealthy thinkers (the more educated) from those who had to earn their living through manual work persist, albeit in a less obvious form given mass education, in the distinction between academic and vocational qualifications. Comprehensive education has removed the physical divide between those aiming for more academic or vocational routes in most of the United Kingdom, but, as Hargreaves points out, the curriculum associated with the grammar school (a school which selects learners on the basis of an ability test and tends to have a more academic curriculum) "continue[s] to hold its central and dominant position in the secondary school curriculum, despite comprehensive reorganization" (Hargreaves, 2012: 51). This means that liberal education is the standard against which individuals are judged and judge themselves, with a more vocational route often perceived as appropriate for the less academically successful, which may, for example, encourage those who would prefer to seek vocational qualifications but come from academic backgrounds to avoid them. Those who are channelled into a vocational pathway may hold negative attitudes about what they perceive to be academic subjects and may struggle with issues of esteem in relation to education. One can distinguish between the overt 'subjects' aspect of the curriculum and the 'hidden' aspect, the latter of which pervades all education systems (Hargreaves, 2012). The hidden curriculum includes unconsciously taught lessons about what we should strive for or fear. In Illich's view, "this hidden curriculum serves as a ritual of initiation into a growth-oriented consumer society for rich and poor alike" (1971: 33).

In short, *education* can have multiple meanings. It encompasses the aims, processes, and outcomes of a system that is underpinned by political objectives, nationally and internationally, which are played out within and beyond educational institutions. The overt curriculum is but a relatively small part of that, one which will increasingly struggle to define what should be learnt when there is so very much that could be included as each moment brings more information. Elements of historic definitions are still relevant today, nonetheless, and so too are the some of the tensions and inequalities that arise from organising learning, in spite of important advances in provision.

Roles, Rights, and Responsibilities

The first question is what part is played by those involved in formal education. Broadly, one could expect the government to make policy, governing bodies and teachers to implement it, parents (by which I mean here and throughout the book those serving a parental role) to support it, and learners to receive it. The implication of this cursory suggestion is that the government and teachers are more active and have more power than parents and learners. In *Parent Power* (Thomson et al., 2009), published by the think tank Reform Scotland, the authors describe the situation in other countries and states, including Nordic countries, where parents do indeed have more power, through choice and the use of voucher schemes. Whilst Thomson et al. say there is much to praise about the Scottish system, there is a call for more parent power through greater choice and the setting up of new schools. The rights afforded to parents differ between countries, thereby restricting or extending the role that parents play. The extent to which parents are held responsible for their children's achievements varies between and within countries. For example, in a comparison of 360 French and 360 English primary school teachers, Broadfoot et al. (1995: 228) found that:

> French teachers . . . take very seriously this perceived responsibility for children's achievement and are more likely than English teachers to express the view that teachers *themselves* must take responsibility for a child's failure rather than blaming it on family background, society etc.

The roles and responsibilities assumed by those in education vary in the extent to which they are explicitly described as opposed to assumed through discourse. Rights are more clearly laid out, although not always fully known or understood. Documentation outlining rights in education include the Equality Act (2010), a document known as the *Burgundy Book* (2000) for Welsh and English schoolteachers, the *Code of Professionalism and Conduct* (2012) for Scottish teachers and the *Code of Values and Professional Practice in Northern Ireland* (2004). These are more about the rights of learners than teachers and refer to the duties and responsibilities of teachers. Rights for teachers include those found in more general employment law and guidance about disciplining young people.

Parents have relatively few rights but play a major role. According to Wilkinson (2001: 232) "parents are the primary educators of their children", although mothers, fathers, guardians, near and distant relatives, siblings and peers should be included in a list of those who contribute to primary socialisation. Parents are responsible for ensuring young people go to school, and Stephen Ball argues persuasively that New Labour—a term to describe the Labour government elected in 2007 under Tony Blair which espoused a free market—promoted the potentially conflicting ideas of 'parent power' and the parental upholding of policy in the 2006 Education Act. As Ball (2008: 179) says, "In the first instance the emphasis is on 'rights' and the second on 'responsibilities'", thereby shifting the burden of outcomes onto what parents do or do not do and away from structural inequalities. This is what Garland refers to, in the context of criminality, as "responsibilization" (1996: 445); similarly, in education, inequality is "posited as cultural and moral rather than structural" (Ball, 2008: 179). The responsibility for education, like criminality, has shifted from the state to individuals and communities, and even more so under the current Conservative–Liberal Democrat coalition government. Free schools are one example of how parents are exercising the right to set up their own state-funded schools in England and Wales following the Academies Act 2010, thereby increasing their responsibility for improved educational outcomes for their children.

Local authorities and councils, parents and teachers have duties as well as responsibilities. *Duty* refers to a legal or moral obligation for which one could be held accountable and therefore responsible. Government acts, for instance, have imposed duties on local authorities regarding the care of children and provision of suitable education in their areas. Schoolteachers in the United Kingdom have a duty of care because of their *in loco parentis* (in place of the parent) role during school hours. Therefore UK teachers' responsibilities include those arising from duty of care for young people up to the age of 18 that are set out in common law laid down by courts, in statutes laid down by the government, and in employment contracts (NUT [National Union of Teachers] Notes 2012–13).

The word *responsibility* has a number of definitions. Here are synonyms taken from a selection of thesauruses: *burden, blame, liability, accountability, constraint, duty,* and *encumbrance.* When *responsibility* is used synonymously with *duty*, it blurs the boundary between what one is obliged to do and what one chooses to take responsibility for when acting autonomously. Admitting responsibility for something can have the implication of fault or of some kind of power. Being responsible can therefore be viewed in a negative, burdensome way (as implied by the majority of synonyms) or in a positive, empowering way. When teachers complain about learners not taking responsibility for their learning, there is the sense that learning is a thing to be done by a particular person and that teachers are being forced into a responsibility that they do not see as theirs, at least not to the extent it is, to ensure student success. Whether teachers view learners taking responsibility as being about reducing their burden or about empowering the student is not always clear.

Outline of Content

Each chapter takes the perspective of one of the main constituents of the education system, that is, those involved in governance, learners, parents and teachers. Some of the main roles, rights and responsibilities are outlined and followed by a review of tensions and inequalities that arise from those. The order of chapters cannot be neutral since one must precede another. I have started with governance because education policy allocates values (Lingard & Ozga, 2007) which those at the receiving end of policy must work with; the other chapters are simply in alphabetical order.

Chapter two takes the perspective of those involved in governance, which includes the minister in charge of education, education departments under that person's leadership, local authorities and governors. Chapter three addresses the roles, rights and responsibilities of learners. The fourth chapter takes the parents' perspective. The fifth chapter shifts to educators and people who provide related services. These include teachers, lecturers, tutors and teaching assistants. The final chapter reviews aspects of the analysis and offers some thoughts on what might be achieved in the future to address some of the points. Throughout the book, the main focus will be on the current situation, although some historical references are included where it is useful to provide some context or to demonstrate consistent tensions or inequalities.

One difficulty in writing about UK education is avoiding a dominant discourse in which England is the "omnipresent reference point" (Phillips, 2000: 10) that leads to talking mainly about the English system and noting 'deviations from the norm' as it were. Another difficulty is the subjectivity of writing as someone with identifiable socioeconomic characteristics, which have no doubt been educationally advantageous at times and disadvantageous at others and influence my understanding, selection and portrayal of material. I am certain that there will be failings in the pages to follow on these counts. To say I have done my best is a philosophically questionable statement, pointed out long ago by Laird (1931). I can only say that I believe that I have done my best to be sensitive to diversity, subjectivity and dominant discourses, an endeavour that in itself is a product of the never-ending process of education.

Chapter Summary

In this chapter I have prepared the ground for the more detailed discussion of roles, rights and responsibilities in the rest of the book. When education in the United Kingdom is discussed in books, journals, policy documents, and the media, it is far from clear which region of the United Kingdom is being referred to. The distinction between English, Welsh, Scottish and Northern Irish education is important because the term *UK* is often used when what is meant is the English system, yet there are important differences between them. Consideration has also been given to the definition of education, revealing that it can refer to both a formal means to acquire knowledge and skills and to lifelong and life-wide learning In this book, the former meaning is predominant. This chapter has provided an overview of roles, rights and responsibilities as well as some illustrative examples of tensions and inequalities that set the scene for what follows. The reader is reminded that the book is, above all, an exploration of the complex education systems in the *United Kingdom* in relation to roles, rights and responsibilities that teases out contemporary dilemmas for all those involved in the structures and processes of learning.

CHAPTER 2

Governance

> **Thinking about Education Governance**
>
> Meg Maguire, Professor of Sociology of Education, King's College, London
>
> What we are currently witnessing in the United Kingdom is a shift away from a welfarist approach to the common good in social policy towards market principles. In these new times, "the geographies of power are shifting" (Robertson & Dale, in Ball, 2013: 222); new stakeholders and power brokers, venture philanthropists and 'edu-businesses' are taking on more responsibilities and power in the educational arena. Groups like Pearson, chains like ARK, agencies like Teach First, and companies like Goldman Sachs (Ball & Junemann, 2012) may, arguably, hold more influence and power to define and influence education policy and practice than government ministers. In these new governance times, we are seeing a shift from the state as locus of power and control to the state as broker, as responsible for "outsourcing, contracting and monitoring" at the same time as it also becomes what Ball (2013: 224) characterises as "extensive, intrusive, surveillant and centred". What is taking place is a shift away from directed forms of government towards a new form of education governance. In this new setting, issues of democratic accountability become *more* rather than *less* pressing.

In terms of governance in the United Kingdom, the picture is made more complex by the shifting set of historical relations and separations between England, Scotland, Wales and Northern Ireland. Thus, different educational states in these national settings will have different perspectives on what policy reforms they may wish to enact. There may also be complex points of distinction in the ways in which market principles have invaded (or not) these national contexts; England, perhaps, is the most radical of the four nations with respect to marketisation and, indeed, forms of privatisation.

What is meant by government and governance is complex and overlapping, and there are distinctions and blurring in these interrelated constructs (Altrichter, 2010). *Governance* generally refers to the exercise of authority in order to manage national affairs. Democratic governance involves establishing some form of legitimacy for enacting reforming tactics (Woods, 2011). However, these interpretations of governance are normative; that is, they present an account of government, and concomitantly governance, as noncontroversial and somewhat inert. What is missing is any question about power relations. Governance takes a variety of forms: it can be deregulated, standardised, or both; it can be tightly or loosely steered; it may involve different forms of privatisation (central and local etc.) Governance may not always take a rational, planned form. As the context shifts, governance (as a form of problem solving) may take the form of rapid-response ways of firefighting.

If we are to research forms of governance, at the very least we need to consider the different perspectives, discourses and *contexts* that shape these sometimes contradictory processes (Altrichter, 2010). For example, the German context is tightly regulated. The role of the state and its capacity for agency is shaped by the constitution, and it enacts laws in such a way that processes of change take longer to work into education provision. The German system, in contrast with the English system, is highly stabilised and rigid to some degree; there is a stronger path dependency here. What we see in England can be described as a thin version of democratic governance—an elected state enacting its manifesto for reform (although the current administration was not actually elected to power). Simultaneously, what we see in the English neoliberal setting is space and autonomy being given to (some) local actors to problem-solve while other stakeholders are tightly regulated—the free schools and academy schools compared with the local-authority community schools, for example. In consequence, it is possible to chart the rise of new networks of policy makers who bypass the usual checks and balances, contexts where tight and loose governance coexist.

Any consideration of governance might also usefully consider questions of governmentality, that is, the ways in which governments 'produce' citizens who are then more likely to enact their policies. Thus, there is a need to know about what McQueen calls 'who does what' in educational policy making—but there is also a need to know a little more about the changes that are taking place in relation to new power brokers, new policy actors and new forms of governance. This need is driven by the principle of democratic accountability; it is about who holds the power to construct a policy problem and shape a policy response (Colebatch, 2006). It is also about who is involved in decision making and the management of change in democratic societies.

The Roles, Rights and Responsibilities of Those in Educational Governance

It is no easy matter to cover the roles, rights and responsibilities of governance in the United Kingdom. This is partly because there are differences in who is in charge of what in the different regions and partly because of the number of agencies involved; these are usually represented by an associated plethora of abbreviations, some of which are acronyms that have taken on a semantic life of their own. For example, *Ofsted* is used so commonly it has turned into a verb in England—'to be ofstedded', meaning inspected—with all the cyclical, angst-ridden and time-consuming implications that brings with it. Another complication in capturing who does what is the number of changes to the names and details of government agencies that have taken place and continue to take place.

There are those who make overarching policy (governmental departments) and those who implement, monitor or regulate it, such as local authorities, senior managers and inspectors, although the government is often involved in these aspects, too. Policy making is the foundation upon which the education system is built. It "shapes who benefits, for what purpose and who pays" (Bell and Stevenson, 2006: 9). Policy must be put into practice, which is the role of a range of other groups and individuals including local education authorities, education managers and teachers. Local policies and practices develop education policy, so it is not just a case of passive implementation (Bell and Stevenson, 2006). As a result, there is scope for differences in how policy is interpreted, for a range of unintended consequences and for considerable diffusion of responsibility.

In 1999, devolution led to the transfer of power to Scotland, Northern Ireland and Wales for policies including education. Some powers are centralised in London, the seat of the UK government, including policies relating to defence and the economy. This is an interesting divide since the economy has become a central theme in education debate and policy making. Alison Wolf commented that "education is big because it is seen as the engine of economic growth, a sure-fire route to future prosperity and victory in a global competition" (2002: x). There is little sign that rhetoric about this drive to be competitive in a global economy, and education's importance to serve it, is decreasing. Indeed, in a recent speech, David Cameron (2013) declared that we are in "an era when global competition and the global race for our economic future has rapidly accelerated . . . there is not a job in the world that doesn't need competent English and competent maths", paving the way to greater emphasis on these subjects in the curriculum, in England in particular. (Obviously there are many jobs in the world that do not require competent skills in English and maths, including in this country.) In other parts of the United Kingdom, the agenda is similarly rooted in the economy, although it can be more nationalistic in essence than global. For example, Education Scotland's website states that:

> Education Scotland is fully committed to ensuring that its activities as a public body make a strong and effective contribution to the Scottish Government's over-arching National Purpose of creating a more successful country with opportunities for all to flourish through sustainable economic growth. (Education Scotland, 2012).

The Northern Ireland Executive Strategy (2011: 31) says, "the need to develop a world class education and skills system is critical for economic growth," and this is reflected in the Department of Education Northern Ireland's corporate goals. The Welsh Department for Education and Skills expresses similar ideas. The emphasis on the economy is a trend that began in the last decades of the twentieth century. As a consequence "a language and practice of managerialism, of accountability, inspection, testing and targets, precluded debates about the purposes of education beyond preparation for the economy" (Tomlinson, 2001: 2).

Alison Wolf, in her book *Does Education Matter?* (2002), argues that pairing education and the economy is problematic, with little evidence to support a direct causal link. Furthermore, she believes that "we impoverish ourselves by our indifference to [cultural, moral and intellectual purposes]" of education (ibid.: 254). Similarly, Stephen Ball (2008) comments on the neglect of social justice in education policy, in spite of some fine words in ministerial speeches. In England in particular, the emphasis on the global economy above all else as justification for policy may serve the purpose of sidestepping underlying awkward cultural, moral and intellectual decisions that are made in a multicultural society. It would be very difficult to present education as the sieving mechanism that it is, sorting individuals for future employment or even likely unemployment, and better to advance the idea that the education system must be structured in a particular way to avoid financial disaster. Gibton (2013: 158), in relation to the role of local authorities but applicable more generally, talks of legislation harnessing "myths to frame problems" in education. The myth here is that the education system is not good enough because the global economy demands certain skills and that it therefore must be changed (again and again). These changes do not tackle the reality that the education system does not provide sufficiently equal opportunities.

The purpose of this chapter is to provide an outline of who does what in the different regions of the United Kingdom, as well as rights afforded and divisions of responsibility. *Governance* is used in the broad sense of those who have the power to influence educational decisions. In principle, this could include parents and students. In practice, these voices, or rather a large proportion of them, have been less influential and remain in the periphery of 'stakeholders'. The first part of the chapter focuses on policy makers, government agencies and stakeholders (see also the chapters on parents and learners), indicating what role each plays. The second part considers some of the tensions and inequalities inherent in the education systems of the United Kingdom, both between and within regions.

Roles

The Role of Central Government and Agencies

It was Bennis (2009) who said that leaders do the right thing while managers do the thing right. The role of those at the top of the governance hierarchy who make policy can be said to be that of the leader who is purportedly doing the right thing for the economy or for any other ideology. Those lower down the hierarchy are given the job of implementing, and less often advising on, policy. The government's role in education, directly or indirectly, includes allocating financial resources, allowing for different types of provision, setting entry requirements, setting fees, and regulating the curriculum and qualifications.

Each region has its own education department:

Scotland	Scottish Government's Education and Lifelong Learning Department
England	(education and children's services) Department for Education (DfE) (higher education) Department for Business Innovation and Skills
N. Ireland	Department of Education Northern Ireland (DENI) (higher education) Department for Employment and Learning
Wales	Department for Education and Skills (Wales) (higher education) Department for Business Innovation and Skills

Ministers are assisted in their policy-making decisions by advisory bodies and individual advisers about whom one hears relatively little. One exception is Charlie Taylor, formerly head of a special school in London and now Chief Executive of the National College for Teaching and Leadership (England and Wales), who has reported on how to manage behaviour in schools and tackle poor attendance (see, e.g., Taylor, 2011).

Since devolution, each governmental department for education provides funding and monitors quality. Some aspects remain shared, however. The Department for Education (England) is responsible for education and children's services in England. Its website refers to working with "nine agencies and public bodies". Those aspects relevant to other parts of the United Kingdom are indicated by the letters *W* (Wales), *NI* (Northern Ireland), and *S* (Scotland). These external agencies and bodies are Ofqual (vocational qualifications NI), Ofsted (the office of Her Majesty's Inspectors [HMI]), the Education Funding Agency, the Standards and Testing Agency, the

National College for Teaching and Leadership, Cafcass, the Office of the Children's Commissioner, the School Teachers' Review Body, and Social Mobility and Child Poverty Commission (W, NI, and S). These agencies vary in their degree of independence and how closely they are involved in education. For example, the Children and Family Court Advisory Service (Cafcass) is an independent agency accountable to the Department for Education (England), although its main role is mediating and advising in court cases involving children's welfare.

Northern Ireland's Education Department (DENI, 2012) states its duties to be the promotion of education in the north of Ireland and to make sure that policy is put into practice effectively. At the time of writing, there are a number of changes taking place. The Education and Skills Authority is being set up, and its role will be to manage the policy made by DENI, including the raising of standards and planning at a local level. It is yet to be decided where the Council for Curriculum, Examinations and Assessment (CCEA) and the inspectorate will be placed. One objective of the Northern Ireland government is to make sure that all children will take part in shared education programme by 2015 (Northern Ireland Executive, 2011), that is, partnerships between schools, in part to reduce the divisions created by parental choice. Another change is that a post-14 Entitlement Framework is now written in law, which requires a broad curriculum that offers young people "access to a coherent and economically relevant choice of courses" (DENI, 2013a).

Wales's Department for Education and Skills has a number of delivery partners. These include childcare providers, schools, school governors, local authorities, Estyn, Colleges Wales, and student representative bodies (Welsh government, 2011a). At the end of the list are children, young people, parents and carers. Unlike other parts of the United Kingdom, Wales is committed to catering for Welsh-language speakers, and policy reflects that commitment. The Welsh assembly government has a Welsh-medium Education Strategy (Welsh government, 2010), partly driven by demand from parents according to the document. Local authorities implement the strategy and are responsible for it.

The Scottish parliament takes the lead in decisions about education in Scotland. State schools are owned and managed by 32 local authorities. Education Scotland is an independent, impartial government "national improvement agency" (Education Scotland, 2012: Foreword), which is accountable to the Scottish government. The Education and Lifelong Learning Department in Scotland has a number of associated agencies, including the Scottish Funding Council (which allocates resources to further and higher education) and the General Teaching Council for Scotland (which monitors the teaching profession). Education Scotland (established in 2011) works in partnership with advisory and monitoring bodies: the Rights, Support and Wellbeing Team, the national CPD (continuing professional development) team, the National Partnership Group, the Research and Innovation team, and HMIs (Her Majesty's Inspectors). Its role is to monitor quality and suggest improvements. Local authorities are important in the education system and are represented by the Convention of Scottish Local Authorities (COSLA), within which the Children and Young People Team leads on education and children's services. Education Scotland and COSLA implement policy and contribute to its development.

Independent bodies monitor standards and qualifications. They also decide which qualifications can be accredited by meeting certain criteria. These are SQA (Scottish Qualifications Authority [Scotland]), CCEA (Council for the Curriculum, Examinations and Assessment [Northern Ireland]), Ofqual (Office of Qualifications and Examinations Regulation [England]), and DCELLS (Department for Children, Education, Lifelong Learning and Skills [Wales]). Scotland has its own qualifications framework (SCQF), while other parts of the United Kingdom share the Qualifications and Credit Framework (QCF). In England, a set of aspirational professional standards for those working in what is sometimes referred to as the postcompulsory or further education or education and training sector have been published in England following the establishment of a new government-funded body, the Education and Training Foundation (ETF, 2014).

Quality of provision is monitored by Her Majesty's Inspectors (HMIs). There are differently named government agencies that oversee standards in care and in education (but not higher education). They are independent of, but funded by, their respective governments, reporting back to them on standards each year. These offices are Estyn (meaning 'to extend'), Ofsted (Office for Standards in Education, Children's Services and Skills [England]), ETI (the Education and Training Inspectorate [Northern Ireland]), and Education Scotland.

The inspection system is complex. For example, some independent schools are inspected by HMIs, but others are inspected by different agencies. The Independent Schools Inspectorate (ISI) is a government-approved body that monitors independent schools belonging to associations that form the Independent Schools Council (approximately 1,200 schools). According to the (English) Department for Education's website, the ISI inspects schools that represent 80 per cent of privately educated students in the United Kingdom. It is unclear whether this is the case because it would appear from reading various sources that the ISI only applies to England. Inspection of independent schools in the rest of the United Kingdom is carried out by HMIs (Estyn, Education Scotland and the ETI). Inspections can also be carried out by the Bridge Schools Inspectorate (BSI). Schools belonging to the Christian Schools' Trust or the Association of Muslim Schools can apply for inspection by the BSI.

The Higher Education Funding Council for England (HEFCE) and for Wales (HEFCW), the Scottish Funding Council (SFC) and DENI distribute government finance to institutions offering higher education courses (universities and some colleges). Quality is monitored through the QAA (Quality Assurance Agency for Higher Education in Northern Ireland, England and Wales). QAA Scotland has a slightly different framework for qualifications "that reflects the features of its different education system [although] they share many core purposes and features" (QAA, 2008: 4).

The Role of Local Governance, Leaders and Stakeholders

National policies are interpreted and acted upon locally. Those whose task it is to turn policy into action include local authorities, governors and institution heads or leaders. These may also influence national policy. The term *stakeholders* is borrowed from business and refers to anyone who has an interest in that business. These may be internal (e.g., teachers and students) or external (e.g., local businesses and other educational organisations).

Local Authorities
The role of local-authority education departments has changed over time and differs between regions. Northern Ireland has five Education and Library Boards (Belfast, northeast, southeast, west, and south) with a local administrative role in each region. The Welsh system has recently been reviewed. The resulting Hill Report (Hill, 2013) judges the present arrangement of local authorities grouped into four consortia (central south Wales, southeast Wales, southwest and mid Wales, and north Wales) to be unsatisfactory because the latter vary in size and because they do not match the division of other services. As a result, there is "confusion of roles and accountabilities" (ibid.: 96) between the consortia and local authorities, with some duplication. Scotland has 32 local authorities, each of which is responsible for education provision locally. The separate authorities work together through COSLA. In England, since the Academies Act (2010), local authorities are only involved with the maintained sector and not with academies (publicly funded independent schools, not to be confused with some Scottish maintained secondary schools called academies). The coalition government has provided for greater institutional autonomy, and thus the role of the local authority is necessarily evolving (Parish et al., 2012).

Higher education institutions (HEIs) are managed separately, although there has been a move towards local economic partnerships (which seem to be synonymous with local enterprise partnerships) between local authorities, universities and businesses with the aim of local economic growth (Local Government Association, 2013). The document refers to the United Kingdom, although the initiative only directly applies to England. The Welsh version of economic enterprise aims "to strengthen the competitiveness of the Welsh economy through Enterprise Zones—not just replicate the approach taken in England" ("Enterprise Zones Wales", 2013). The zones are more specialist, each concentrating on one economic aspect.

Governors
(See also chapter 4 for parent governors.)
School affairs are overseen by a group of parents, teachers and other stakeholders. These are known as governors in England, Wales and Northern Ireland. In Scotland, school boards were established in 1988 (School Boards [Scotland] Act, 1988), whereas in the rest of the United Kingdom school boards have been abolished in favour of governance by local authorities and governing bodies. The roles in the different regions are similar and broadly involve monitoring school processes, acting as a link between the school and parents, and reporting to parents.

The head teacher may or may not be a member of the board, depending on the region. Students are usually not part of a governing body except in Wales, which has associate pupil governors (Governors Wales, 2013). Scottish school boards consist of parents and teachers as well as co-opted members as appropriate. They monitor how school funds are spent as well as policies relating to discipline, the curriculum and assessment. They also promote good relations between parents and staff. Northern Ireland emphasises parents less. Indeed the subheading of DENI's leaflet, *Becoming a School Governor* (2013–2014), is "for people from all walks of life". The leaflet also states that governors are not education experts but that they work in partnership with the school for quality (standards) purposes.

England's conservative-liberal democratic coalition government, which formed following the 2010 election, wrote a white paper that planned to increase local autonomy for schools. In the process of decentralisation, the role of Ofsted and local governors was highlighted as central to accountability. School governors, the paper says, "are the unsung heroes of our education system. They are one of the biggest volunteer forces in the country, working in their spare time to promote school improvement and to support head teachers and teachers in their work" (Department for Education, 2010: 71).

Since the Further and Higher Education Act (1992), further education colleges have been incorporated in England and Wales, a process that freed them from local-authority control. In Scotland, a parallel system was set up at that time. Each college is overseen by a board of management (Audit Scotland, 2012). The role of those on boards of management may not be clearly understood, Griggs (2012: 18) suggests in his report. "As one auditor said to us he believes that the FE Sector has some of the best Non Executives across the public sector but some of the least understanding in governance terms of what they are there to do, and of their responsibilities". In Northern Ireland colleges were taken out of Education and Library Board control in 1997. There are now six governing bodies that reflect the merger of 16 colleges of further education in 2007. The purpose of the governors is to make sure that students receive a "suitable and efficient" education (Department for Employment and Learning, 2008: 12).

Generally speaking, further and higher education governors have a similar role to school and college governors, overseeing standards and monitoring finances. In higher education there are some regional variations that are laid out in the guide for members of higher education governing bodies (Department for Education, 2010). One duty of higher education governors is to approve the tuition fees set by institutions, which since their introduction in England, Wales and Northern Ireland have mostly been set at the maximum permitted (Committee of University Chairs, 2009–2014). At present, Scotland only charges non-EU and non-Scottish UK students for tuition.

Head Teachers, School Leaders, Principals and Vice-Chancellors, and Senior Management

The terms *head teacher*, *school leader*, *principal*, and *director* are often used interchangeably to mean the person at the top of the hierarchy of an institution's leadership. It is usual to hear the term *principal* for further education leaders. Headmasters and headmistresses, as they were once called, did teach, although a limited amount. Now head teachers may not teach at all, so extensive is their management role. This is particularly true of university vice-chancellors (VCs). (The chancellor of a university, incidentally, is a leader in an official or ceremonial but not practical capacity.) Sir David Bell, VC of Reading University, recently likened his role to "running a small town" (BBC News, October 10, 2013).

Earley et al. (2011) report research into the role of school leaders in cities; adjectives used to describe the role include *fast-paced, stressful, relentless, fragmented, complex* and *emotionally demanding*. Head teachers may be somewhat isolated in their role and are likely to do "walkabouts" (ibid.: 6; more often called "learning walks") so that they are seen as accessible and to remain in contact with those whom they manage. Bristow et al. (2007, cited in Earley et al., 2011) categorised 54 activities into five main areas: leadership, management, administration, teaching and continuous professional development. A study carried out in Scotland by MacBeath et al. (2009) indicated that a head teacher's role could be divided into two areas: strategic leadership and leadership of personnel, with the former taking precedence but the latter providing more satisfaction. The sample of 178 head teachers interviewed, drawn from primary, secondary and special schools, expressed dislike for the "excessive and often unnecessary" paperwork (ibid.: 25).

Each institutional leader is supported by a senior management team (SMT). The other team members may have a teaching role, although this is less likely in further and higher education. Indeed, senior managers may have neither teaching experience nor teaching qualification and will have been appointed because of their experience in managing noneducational organisations. This fact demonstrates the extent to which education has become a business.

Senior managers have a strategic role to play in education. Keating and Moorcroft (2006) say that strategy can be defined in terms of design, experience and ideas, principles that can be applied to all education institutions. The first of these relates to a "planning school" (ibid.: 131) that rationally considers the direction the school is taking, analysing and evaluating how the school (or indeed college or university) responds to internal and external challenges. Strategy as experience involves more reflection than rationalisation and includes not just what must be done but how to do it. In schools, business managers may be employed, leaving other senior managers to focus on teaching and learning. The experience strategy is more bottom-up than top-down, which may lead to a more unique approach to managing an organisation. The authors comment:

Some professional organisations (notably universities) have been characterised as organised anarchies where intelligent, strong-willed professionals pursue local goals and values that may be disconnected from the official mission statement and strategic priorities. (139)

The final strategy is founded on ideas. In this sense, "the central task of the senior leaders within a school is to define, through consultation, the core values of their organisation and its overall vision or mission" (ibid.: 140). Management that takes this approach will encourage an open discussion of educational matters rather than dictate solutions.

Stakeholders

The word *stakeholders* is used throughout the United Kingdom today without much thought, just as the word *teachers* might be, when talking about education. However, it was unheard of before education became equated with business in the 1980s. Stakeholder theory was developed by Freeman at that time. He says that "organizations have stakeholders. That is, there are groups and individuals who can affect, or are affected by, the achievement of an organization's mission" (Freeman, 2010: 52, first published in 1984). Narrow stakeholders are those immediately affected by an organisation (for instance, students and teachers), whereas wide stakeholders are indirectly influenced (for instance, local businesses and others in the community). According to this framework, organisations must respond to stakeholders. There is a "need for processes and techniques to enhance the strategic management capability of the organization" (ibid.: 53).

The idea of stakeholder involvement is that they form part of a network of interested parties. In theory their role is to support innovation and development or to challenge and to offer innovative ideas (Hopkins, 2003). In practice, stakeholders may refer to a very limited set of individuals and organisations. Parents (other than governors) and students have much less influence than those directly involved in education such as principals, teachers and perhaps education researchers. For example, assuming no error, Devon County Council's Infrastructure Plan (2013) refers to "stakeholders, partners, parents, young people, local community".

This implies that there are key stakeholders, such as head teachers, senior managers and governors, who are more influential.

Concluding Comments

This rather brief outline of who does what demonstrates that education departments in each region of the United Kingdom have slightly different roles, with Scotland, for example, having a more centralised one than England. It also indicates what a large-scale and unwieldy project education is in the United Kingdom. The central place of education in government rhetoric, particularly in England, to solve economic ills has been referred to. Indeed Bell and Stephenson (2006) say that an important role of the state is to encourage dominant discourses so that the populous (or voters) support decisions in the belief that there could be no rational alternative given particular social or economic conditions. It also highlights that education is a business that demands continual planning and strategic management by all levels of governance to keep pace with shifting political emphases and the ever-present requirement for accountability. Change has reached pathological proportions in education (called a "policy epidemic" by Levin, 1998: 137, and "initiativitis" by Ball et al., 2012: 141)—a situation in which those in charge can be seen as both the cause and the hoped-for cure for perceived educational ills.

Rights

This section is brief and covers all those referred to under "Roles". Its brevity reflects the fact that those in governance or associated agencies have or are given certain powers, which are often equivalent to rights. Rights are rarely referred to specifically. For example, the rights of the government to change educational policy are constrained only by democratic processes, particularly the desire to remain in power, and by acceptance of international and European statements of human rights. The latter has been the subject of considerable debate in recent years (see, e.g., Maer & Horne, 2009) with a call for a British bill of rights. Even if this were to come about, it would have little effect on governmental rights in relation to education. In general, the duties that have been given by the government to other agencies are requirements that give those agencies, in effect, a right to certain actions, some of which are ensuring that human rights are implemented by the institutions they are involved with, or to information. One specific right is that of Her Majesty's Inspectors, who have right of access to education providers for inspection purposes.

Responsibility

It is important here to refer to the notions of responsibility and accountability and to the point that both of these are difficult to separate from roles in many instances. The government is responsible for making policy but can claim much less or no responsibility for its implementation. It is less directly accountable than, for example, local authorities, education institution management or teachers. The government's role is to manage its nation's affairs, which confers an obligation to monitor systems, including education. It is not obliged to change those systems, although it often does for national or international ideological reasons. A new government provides the opportunity to make changes at election times that purportedly respond to voters' discontent or to economic concerns. However, there are no data available in England to support the rhetoric that parents want more choice yet that was the basis (in rhetoric) for the introduction of free schools.

In its 2010 manifesto, the conservative party opened its political arguments with this question: "How can we take Britain in a completely new direction?" (*The Conservative Government Quality of Life Manifesto*, 2010: 3). In education, its answer (for England rather than Britain) was to veer away from state-led education towards community-led education (particularly free schools). By so doing, the government held the outgoing Labour Party to be accountable for problems with inequity or poor standards. Now in opposition, the Labour Party and indeed the Liberal Democrats as part of the coalition government have questioned the free-school agenda (recent concerns have been misuse of funds [*The Guardian*, October 25, 2013] and the legitimate employment of unqualified teachers [*The Independent*, 2013]), but the government can claim that individual schools are to blame for problems and not the policy (see, e.g., Hansard, October 17, 2013). During the debate, David Laws (minister of state for schools in England) deflected responsibility and responded to questions about the appropriateness of employing unqualified teachers thus: "The governing body and the school leadership have a clear responsibility to recruit teachers who are fit to do the job" (ibid.: column 892).

There is much wriggle room in a multiagency system, particularly for those who hold the most or least power. In education the government and inspectors at one end and learners at the other tend to be held less responsible than agencies or other stakeholders, including local authorities and teachers. Bivins (2006) discusses responsibility, accountability and autonomy in relation to public relations, making points that are relevant to education, too. He concludes:

> We must realize that not every actor is blameworthy, especially if the actor's autonomy is limited by structure, process, or circumstance. Likewise, accountability for actions may be lessened as autonomy is eroded by either role or environment. (38)

Education policy is responsible for structure and to some extent process. Notwithstanding limits imposed by circumstances, there is still considerable autonomy in devising local policy. In the process, a government can distance itself from responsibility. Thus, in England, "the devolution of choice to parents and autonomy to educational institutions is used by many policy makers to hold to account those responsible for the work of those institutions." (Bell & Stevenson, 2006: 39). Of course accountability can encourage self-improvement, which is often the case informally. Gilbert (2012) argues for a rebalancing of quality monitoring so that schools are, in effect, their own judges within an inspection framework. Such an approach formalises the professional evaluation that educators often undertake in order to do the best for their students.

Consideration of who is responsible for what, beyond the duties that a role confers, brings to the fore some difficult issues for the education system. Responsibility and accountability are so widely spread across education systems that addressing why an individual student or indeed an institution has not succeeded makes it difficult to pin down any one factor. Students may have some responsibility for outcomes, but they can hardly be held accountable. Those in governance who hold others to account tend not to be accountable, which includes policy makers, inspectors and governors.

For example, inspectors are responsible for monitoring the quality of schools, colleges and teacher training but not for deciding the policy that sets educational priorities or, for the most part, how to address perceived failings, assuming that inspection grading can be relied upon. Management is likely to be seen as responsible for shortcomings, even if they are just inadequate managers of the inspection process. There has also been debate amongst ministers in England as to the independence of the inspectorate, which on one occasion was referred to as "cosy with the government" and "its poodle" because of Ofsted's involvement in the development of a report card for schools (*The Telegraph*, 2009). However, more recently, there has been a furore over the sacking of the chair of Ofsted, Lady Morgan, who is a Labour peer (BBC News, February 12, 2014), not long after the chief inspectors of schools for England, Sir Michael Wilshaw, angrily responded to the possibility that Michael Gove might wish to scrap Ofsted altogether (BBC News, January 26, 2014). In short, these events imply a complex relationship between government and inspection agencies.

A second example is that governors have a wide range of responsibilities relating to a school's performance (see, e.g., Department for Education, 2014a; Taverner, 1994). However, although governors hold schools to account, they are very rarely seen to be responsible for shortcomings. An example of where governors were blamed for a failing school was in Wales in 2012, and since then the education minister has approved the dismissal of the governing body, which has been replaced with an interim and shadowing body (Cardiff Council, 2013).

A final example is that exam boards are responsible for setting and marking exams yet those regulating assessment may overrule grading. This led to the controversy in England over altered grade boundaries in 2013 in English GCSEs (*Times Educational*

Supplement, leaked letters, 2012). Ofqual was acting within its responsibility for regulating assessment standards, although questions about how independent it is when it must serve the government's agenda were raised from its inception in 2008.

It is particularly evident in England that responsibility has shifted away from the centre for the success or otherwise of education providers in each community; "increasingly, education is being treated as a private good rather than a public responsibility" (Whitty & Power, 2000: 105). Scotland (and to some extent Northern Ireland and Wales) relies more on local authorities; these therefore have greater responsibilities. The Welsh government has responded to the Hill Report (2013) by picking two of the recommendations, one of which is to remove responsibility for school improvement services from local authorities. However, such tweaking of responsibilities is unlikely to make a fundamental difference to the educational experience of the majority of learners. The shadow education minister, Simon Thomas, called this response a "damp squib" and claimed that he would call the local-authority consortia to account by chairing meetings with them to improve accountability (Plaid Cymru, 2013).

National governments' power to alter the roles and responsibilities of those who implement policy and monitor the effects to ensure constant improvement, in itself an ill-defined and thus impossible target the moment one looks beyond exam results, is one that should be exercised with greater caution. In spite of a plethora of changes in the past three decades in particular, many schools remain 'not good enough'. In addition, moving roles and associated responsibilities around, sometimes by closing and opening various agencies, creates a stressful work environment that cannot be conducive to sustained and sustainable improvement. The emphasis on change, improvement and efficiency adds to stress throughout the system, including higher education (see, e.g., Tytherleigh et al., 2005).

Tensions

A number of tensions are evident in the education systems of the United Kingdom. Some apply to the whole of the United Kingdom and others to particular regions. Policy making is a site of tension

(Garratt & Forrester, 2012). There will inevitably be disagreement about education policy, nationally and locally regarding both its content and its interpretation. A pluralist model of policy making uses democratic principles to include majority views. Policy makers find ways to produce policy that can be applied to different viewpoints. This may be one reason why government acts consist of many general statements. "Tensions between social groupings are not denied within the pluralist model, on the contrary, the state is seen as having a key role in reconciling conflicting interests" (Bell & Stevenson, 2006: 27). However, much recent policy in England can be seen as elitism dressed in pluralist clothing.

Neoliberalism, Choice and Social Unity

In all parts of the United Kingdom, education policy makers and educational leaders are struggling with issues of choice, maintenance of traditions, meeting the needs of socially diverse populations, and fostering a tolerant, socially unified and egalitarian society. As long as education is a breeding ground for social competition, equality of provision and outcome will be problematic. As Ward and Eden (2009: 37) point out, "comprehensive schooling increased, rather than diminished, inequality" because of middle-class parents' ability to play the system. The introduction of free schools in England, the continuing policy of selective education in parts of the United Kingdom, and the long-standing tradition of faith schools in all of the United Kingdom only serve to increase opportunities for inequality.

Looking back to the landmark Education Act of 1944 (the Butler Act for England and Wales, with similar acts for Scotland and Northern Ireland shortly after), which secured free secondary education in the United Kingdom, there was in the end widespread acceptance of it by different political parties. However, aside from considerable debate generally in Parliament prior to this major change, Barber refers to the "tortuous negotiations" (1994: 50) that took place with Anglican, Catholic and Non-conformist churches. The demand for faith schools, and for funding for them, has persisted. According to the British Humanist Association (BHA, 2012), the government has not been keeping records of the number of applications for free schools from different religious groups. The association's own research indicates that the majority are from religious or pseudoscientific organisations, although many of these applications have been rejected.

Some of the difficulties associated with opening the doors to multiple types of school, whether faith or not, have become apparent recently in England but are neither new nor unexpected, given existing tensions or indeed logical thought. Problems that have made the headlines recently include poor standards (BBC News, October 15, 2013), yet one of David Cameron's arguments for faith schools was that they would improve standards (*The Telegraph*, January 26, 2010). There is, then, a tension between maintaining national standards and permitting self-management, the latter allowing for autonomous and different approaches to what is considered acceptable. On the other hand, independent schools and the schools that David Cameron was probably thinking of, such as the "excellent Church of England school" (ibid.) that his daughter attended, indicate that independence and quality are not necessarily incompatible but depend on acceptance of particular cultural standards. Many established schools are of course chosen not for their religious affiliation but for their results (Westminster Faith Debates, 2013).

In Scotland, the Catholic religion is dominant in faith schools. Forty per cent of primary school pupils in Glasgow attend a Catholic school (Riddell et al., 2009). Of the 377 publicly funded faith schools, 374 are Catholic (Scottish government, 2011). There are no league tables for Scotland and no national testing prior to public examinations, and the latter differs from other parts of the United Kingdom; therefore it is difficult to comment on standards between schools or between regions. One issue for Scotland is maintaining its educational tradition of democracy, equality and social unity, although this tradition is both "amorphous" and somewhat mythical (Bryce & Humes, 2006: 33). In an increasingly multicultural society, and one that embraces choice, social unity sits uncomfortably at times with sectarian choices, whether on religious or academic grounds.

Welsh students on average achieve lower grades in public exams (GCSE and A-level) than English students (Hill, 2013). In his report, Robert Hill (2013) indicates that there is a problem with the strategic approach to managing education:

> Schools must take responsibility for their own improvement and foster a culture of open classrooms where teachers can observe and learn from each other's practice as a matter of course. The role of school leaders should be focused not on meetings and administration but on instruction and supporting improvement in the classroom. (6)

He calls for a more collaborative approach with strong leadership, including by teachers, and the formation of partnerships. What prevents this, he says, is over-dependence on local authorities, particularly by primary schools, with a number of local authorities judged by Estyn to be inadequate.

Northern Ireland has to contend with a selective, religiously sectarian, and dual-language system. Since 2008, it has been up to families to decide whether children are entered for the selection exam. The original suggestion that there should be no selection was resisted by some politicians, grammar schools and parents, and a nonstatutory form of selection remains. Research indicates advantages for those attending grammar schools, which includes higher status, esteem, achievement and aspirations (Gallagher & Smith, 2000). Staff are also affected by the social implications of school difference (ibid.), with some secondary school teachers opting for a selective school for their own children and feeling guilty about having double standards. Social differences and inequality are also evident in Catholic and Irish medium schools where the proportion of children entitled to free school meals (as a measure of socio-economic disadvantage) is higher (Lundy et al., 2013). Government policy has promoted integrated schooling, although the first integrated school was set up by parents in Belfast in 1981 (McGlynn, 2004). Compared with the rest of the United Kingdom, Northern Ireland has done more to tackle social division, given the civil unrest it has experienced. Integrated schools are one measure, the others being the Education for Mutual Understanding curriculum and school contact programmes. However, only 7 per cent of learners attend integrated schools (DENI, 2013b). Gallagher proposes that "the problems of a divided society will only be addressed if they are constantly and explicitly being addressed" (2004: 130). In other parts of the United Kingdom, these problems may well be underestimated. Increasing choice will be insufficient to combat social tensions and may lead to greater inequality (see, e.g., Orfield & Frankenberg, 2013).

As Hill says in relation to Wales:

> The accountability system needs to balance the tension between competition and collaboration which is inherent in a more autonomous system. Measures may be needed to ensure that schools serving disadvantaged students are not adversely affected by greater autonomy and choice. (2013: 54).

Equity and Efficiency

An efficient system can sit uncomfortably with equity, if the latter is taken to mean equal opportunity, equal provision or equal choice. The word *efficiency* is referred to 90 times in one of the English government's documents and is fundamentally connected to strategic management of finances and its relationship with success rates. "A key to efficiency is how schools spend the money they have available, not just how much they spend" (Department for Education, 2013a: 6). Although calling for greater autonomy for schools in financial regulation, there will remain the issue of trust since wasting public funds "is not acceptable" (ibid.: 7) and will need to be checked against criteria of acceptability, one assumes.

Efficiency is basically a cost-benefit analysis whereby an efficient education system has maximum output in relation to a particular input. The outputs are specified by any given system and could be qualifications or employability (Wößmann & Schütz, 2006). There are other possible outputs that improve quality of life, such as health. Equity relates to fairness and social justice, although the definition of the latter may not be agreed upon. A generally agreed-upon definition might be this:

> The concept of equity understood in terms of equality of opportunity would call for an equal access to education and training

programmes independent of students' circumstances, as well as for an equal treatment of all students independent of their circumstances. At the same time, this concept of equity would not necessarily call for a strict equality of educational outcomes in the sense of a perfect sameness or egalitarianism, because people are allowed to choose to differ according to their self-determined effort. (ibid.: 3)

It could be assumed that efficiency is desirable because wasting resources will have a negative effect on those for whom social justice is sought. Research, mostly in the United States, indicates that investment early on in a person's life has substantial benefits later on, the lack of which is more costly and difficult to remedy (ibid.). Investment outside the education system is important, too, however. Education is not a cure-all.

An equity-efficiency analysis assumes a deficit model whereby society must put right the effects of unequal living circumstances. To be competitive within the system that exists, that may well be the logical conclusion. However, even if it were possible to reduce all output to effort, surely it would not be possible for all in society to have the increased benefit that derives from society's inequality of income. This is possible if the United Kingdom or any other country benefits from, or rather exploits, the relative poverty of other countries instead of its own population. An efficient and equitable system will be a trade-off at some level.

Inequalities

Those in governance are well aware of systematic inequalities in education throughout the United Kingdom. Education Scotland refers to inequality as remaining a major challenge; in Northern Ireland those subject to poor outcomes include Protestant working-class boys, the Traveller community, carers, those with disabilities and ethnic minorities (DENI, Audit 2012); and in Wales, those with special educational needs or disabilities, Travellers, white working-class boys and some ethnic minority pupils (not Chinese, for example) fare worse (Welsh government, 2013). Michael Gove (2010) highlighted difficulties in England in a speech to a private school:

> We live in a profoundly unequal society. More than almost any developed nation ours is a country in which your parentage dictates your progress. Those who are born poor are more likely to stay poor and those who inherit privilege are more likely to pass on privilege in England than in any comparable county. For those of us who believe in social justice this stratification and segregation are morally indefensible.

Policy documents often comment on the progress that has been made (by those currently in governance) although they also state that there is still work to do. Poverty is cited as an underlying cause regardless of other differences between learners. For example, Wales has "pockets of wealth and swathes of poverty" (Jones & Roderick, 2003: 2). There is a significant relationship between poverty and low achievement, although it is not the only factor. Apart from poverty, causes include low parental expectations, negative experiences (e.g., racism and bullying), and teacher bias. There is evidence that some ethnic minorities are disadvantaged regardless of socio-economic status or gender (Gillborn & Mirza, 2000). A difficulty with deciphering inequality is that there are combined effects so that an identified inequality, such as gender, combines with other characteristics or experiences, thereby conflating different social disadvantages (Lynch & Lodge, 2002).

Initiatives to tackle underachievement often only address poverty indirectly through improving the economy by changing education for the current economic climate. The changes suggested or implemented include raising and monitoring standards, tackling disruptive behaviour more robustly and increasing autonomy in education. There is some evidence that parental involvement is one of the best ways to reduce the gap in attainment (Carter-Wall & Whitfield, 2012) if more microlevel strategies are adopted.

If adapting the present education system, then an inclusive strategy is called for to combat systemic and sustained unequal access and treatment. This would seem to be at odds with the path taken in England, down which lies greater inequality through the right to choose, which is likely to widen rather than narrow the gap between the rich and poor as well as to exacerbate difference (as has been found in Northern Ireland). It is not poverty alone that is the cause of many ills, according to Wilkinson and Pickett (2009), but the degree of difference in wealth. Countries such as the United Kingdom, the United States, and Singapore, where there is a large gap between the rich and poor, have more health and social problems than more equal countries such as Japan and Sweden.

Another suggestion to improve equality is through recognition. The argument is that some groups are more recognised by society than others. Whether by intention or through lack of thought, some individuals are not recognised or are misrecognised through their association with a particular, nondominant group (Lynch & Lodge, 2002). In Scotland, for instance, older people in some rural areas and Muslims need greater consideration to make sure that health and education takes their needs into account (Equality and Human Rights Commission, 2010). The theme of recognition will be returned to in the final chapter. The point here is that those in governance, according to the recognition analysis, must ensure no one is excluded from policy at all levels. Free schools could be interpreted as opportunities for all those lacking recognition to develop their own education opportunities. In reality, those who already have recognition are more likely to succeed. Another type of recognition is institutional, which might lead to misrecognition if information is inaccurate or biased. Scotland has avoided using league tables, which may be beneficial in sidestepping the difficulty of negative messages about schools, for instance. Again, those that are 'recognised' have an advantage.

> While some may be able to leave the 'sinking ship', the most disadvantaged will rarely have that option. They may find themselves trapped in a spiral of institutional and aspirational decline. (Power & Frandji, 2010: 389)

However, rather than focusing on differences between institutions, which league tables encourage, it is instructive to bear in mind the greater similarities. Statistically, there is not that much difference between outcomes from different institutions (Wiliam, 2012), where data are comparable.

Policy makers are central to the education system and to the structures that manage and monitor the implementation of their endeavours. All parts of the United Kingdom have adopted neo-liberal strategies, although there are pockets of resistance in Scotland. Governments continue to review the education system and to tweak various aspects of it. There is a joke about asking for directions and getting the reply 'Well, I wouldn't start from here'. There is no choice but to start from where we are in education, although that does not mean that what follows must be similar to current or past versions. Before the Butler Act, only the privileged in the United Kingdom benefited from being formally educated. Now only the privileged benefit from particular forms of education. The fine detail of who benefits and who does not may change over time, but fundamental inequalities do not. This is because education alone cannot change entrenched inequalities. Throughout the United Kingdom, "the articulation of rights and responsibilities presumes a liberal understanding that all individuals qua citizens are equal and all communities are unimpeded by structural inequalities" (Garratt & Forrester, 2012: 27).

Chapter Summary

The overview of those who govern education in this chapter indicates that there are many and varied individuals and groups involved. These include business organisations, as Meg Maguire indicates in her preface. Those in governance have a large role in shaping the education policies and systems in place, whether at a national or local level. National policy has increasingly emphasised the requirement for education to solve economic difficulties to the point that other educational goals have been obscured or exist in tension with the demand for high performance through national tests and exams. Monitoring of performance pervades education, although some aspects, such as inspections, vary in the methods used and the amount of tension they create. The large role of national governance is matched by extensive but unformulated rights to alter an education system to suit political goals with little restriction other than the desire to be re-elected. The right to change the system would make those in governance responsible if it were an easier matter than it is to demonstrate that policies are the cause of low achievement or inequality or any other educational malaise. As a result, those who are held to account for failings tend to be managers, teachers, parents and, less often, learners. Tensions that are strongly felt include how to manage social unity within a system of choice and how to balance equity and efficiency. The chapter ends by considering the effect of inequality on educational choices and outcomes, which is one consequence of the wide gap between rich and poor in the United Kingdom.

CHAPTER 3

Learners

Rebalancing the Learner-Teacher Partnership

John Webber, Professional Learning and Development Manager, Sussex Downs College, East Sussex

The increasing pressure placed on educational providers, in particular colleges and universities, to consult and respond to 'learner voice' coincides with, and arguably forms part of, the developing identity of the learner as a customer. Whilst one might hope that this could help address the issue of learners' rights, there is a risk that it can lead to a misunderstanding of the learner's role and run contrary to the learner recognising his or her responsibilities in relation to learning. Indeed, there is a risk that the 'customer satisfaction' aspect of quality assurance might lead to distortions to practice that undermine real learning and hence eventually also deny the learners their rights to this.

For this and other reasons, I find this chapter, and indeed McQueen's wider discussion of roles, rights and responsibilities, both timely and helpful. In this short response I will attempt to bring out some of the ways her analysis relates to challenges we have met within a large and diverse further education college. The discussion of the multiple dichotomies such as active-passive, autonomous-dependent and expert-novice is particularly relevant.

These dichotomies came into sharp focus four years ago following concerns raised by the curriculum leader and head of English about both the low value many learners placed on homework as formative assessment and their lack of engagement or ability to respond to feedback on marked work. Interviews with students, both within this cohort and elsewhere in the college, revealed that many saw homework as something you do to please the teacher or at least to keep the teacher off your back. They saw written feedback as the teacher's part of the contract but not something of any real interest, unless it was on a draft piece of work with clear directions on how to get a higher mark. As the research reported by Dylan Wiliam and Paul Black (see, e.g., Wiliam, 2011) predicted, grades absorbed the interest of learners and, once they entered the transaction, little else mattered.

In a parallel focus group, teachers claimed that learners were increasingly ill prepared for the independent learning expected of them at college because of the 'grade-farming' in schools in the run up to GCSEs. As we probed further, it became apparent that it was all too easy for teachers and students to be drawn into unconscious collusion, recreating the 'spoon-feeding' that both parties disparaged. This finding was echoed in a report by Cambridge Assessment on the views of university lecturers (Mehta et al., 2012). It appears that within a culture which emphasises graded outcomes as the primary measure of success for learners and their teachers, shortcuts to achievement, with minimal challenge, become attractive to both parties. This led us to focus on the development of effective 'studentship' (i.e. the behaviours, skills, personal attributes and beliefs that enable effective learning) as a goal to be valued both for its importance to students' learning whilst at college and as a preparation for work or further study.

It appeared that we were pushing at an open door. Students interviewed during induction to college identified increased independence and 'freedom' as key differences that they anticipated enjoying. However, interviewed again later in the year, it was evident that many found greater independence to be challenging, both practically and psychologically. The words of one learner who struggled with the transition echo the feelings of many: "At school you were aware that teachers were there to get you through the exams whereas here teachers want to help you but it's up to you."

Perhaps we shouldn't be surprised. Growing to an adult acceptance of independence and self-responsibility is a much more complex and ambivalent process than the initial prospect of freedom appears to adolescent eyes. Where there is an institutionalised fear of failure and consequent distrust of innovation evident in the conservative practice of many teachers and students, this can readily lead to reinstating the teacher as the authority responsible for learning and the student as a passive recipient. If you had to choose between good grades and deep learning strategies, then what would your choice be?

However, we are also finding, through a variety of supported experiments within our college, that there are many practical ways by which teachers can cut through this Gordian knot. 'Flipped learning' enables students to secure basic knowledge before they come to class, thus freeing up class time for deeper engagement. Effective peer- and self-assessment can raise aspirations and empower students to engage more effectively with the criteria for higher grades. Creating a culture that fosters peer teaching and collaborative learning builds confidence and encourages active engagement. All offer ways of both improving outcomes whilst empowering students and enhancing the quality of learning (see, e.g., Coffield et al., 2014, for a fuller exploration of these approaches). The research evidence confirms the effectiveness of these approaches, but their wider adoption requires deep shifts in the beliefs about effective learning that are held by institutions, teachers and learners alike. It is to be hoped that this book will contribute to addressing that requirement.

This chapter focuses on learners, the word chosen to describe anyone who chooses or is expected to learn in a given situation. Other terms, such as *student, pupil* or *apprentice*, tend to be used in particular contexts. Respectively these are college and university (sometimes school), school and work-based learning. However, it is acknowledged that any term fails to capture the complex social meaning attached to the role. Much theory and literature focuses more on the characteristics, experiences and outcomes of learners, as well as on theory of how people learn either as individuals or in social contexts, than on what they do. One difficulty with asking what learners do is that actions are a response to what they have been told, encouraged, expected or asked to do; the roles of governance, parents and teachers are therefore implicated.

What do learners do? The obvious response is that they learn. However, that is not necessarily the case, or at least they may not be learning what was intended. In addition, the effect of multiple social roles of learners on the capacity to be a learner in a normative, traditional sense can be underestimated. For example, the 2011 census indicated that there are 166,000 children acting as carers for a family member in England (The Children's Society, 2013). Another important question is whether learners do the same thing at different ages or if their role changes over time. For example, adult learners might have a very different role from that of children in preschool. There is no simple answer to this because as soon as a learner is placed in an institutional setting or provided with a curriculum to follow or with learning materials, that person becomes part of complex interactions both between people and between a person and written or spoken information. These interactions influence the role that is taken.

Osler and Flack (2008) began to recognise ways in which they, as teachers, were inadvertently disempowering students through unquestioningly responding to demands for help, which can occur regardless of the age of learners. These roles are rendered normal by other social relationships (for instance, adult-child) in which the learner is placed in a subordinate role, one that may continue into further, higher and adult education. However, it might equally be suggested that the learners had learnt how to gain attention from their teachers—by acting helplessly. Teachers might feel rewarded by assuming that they are being useful and helpful. In addition, the hierarchical structure might seem appropriate in society, thereby indicating that teachers are encouraging appropriate behaviour. Swann (2013: 6) says the following about schools:

> To various degrees all schools impart some form of social role in relation to their pupils. By virtue of its purposes and procedures, schooling is inescapably committed to transcend the interests of the individual for the greater good of ensuring that children's behaviour is consistent with general societal expectations so that they make a positive contribution to society overall.

The ethos of any institution is highly influential in determining the part played by learners and the subsequent outcomes. This institutional character is dependent not just on the top-down influence of educators, I would argue, but also on those who are classed as learners, because of the reciprocal nature of interactions. The normative behaviour and expectations of learners within a community, and consequently the response of an institution, are important in constructing which policies and practices are established or enforced. Consider the following: A social experiment called *Second Chance* was broadcast on Channel 4 in 2002. A black teenager from London who had been expelled from school for, in short, non-compliant behaviour was given the chance to study at Downside, a Catholic private school. Initially the experiment "succeeded beyond any expectations" (*The Telegraph*, 2002). However, he was later expelled from Downside for getting drunk. The young man, who has since gained one A-level at a private tutorial college, having excelled in Latin and rugby whilst at Downside, now has high aspirations for his daughter and reads to her regularly (*Daily Mail* online, 2009), which might be considered a silver lining to a clouded experience. Compare this with the fate of Euan Blair, son of former prime minister Tony Blair, whose much more public and widely reported misdemeanour of getting drunk in Trafalgar Square when celebrating his GCSE results, did not stand in the way of being made deputy head boy in the sixth form or of going to university (*The Telegraph*, 2001). Although the latter incident took place when the exams had finished, it would be impossible for the sixth form institution to be unaware of what had occurred. It is the role of institutions, therefore, to designate behaviour to a category, such as deviance or silliness, which can be a life-changing difference.

It became apparent when researching for this chapter that the role of a learner plays out on a number of continua—for example, active-passive. Learners cannot be positioned consistently in one place on a continuum; different teachers, subjects, life events and other contextual factors can move a learner from one point to another. It is also the case that perceptions of learners result in others positioning them on a continuum. These perceptions may or may not be accurate. For example, someone with a learning difficulty might be viewed erroneously as more dependent than autonomous. Thus attributions of ability, character or intention assign certain roles. Teachers quite often have to act as judge and jury when incidences arise, deciding who did what to whom and why. For instance, Lines (2008) describes the complexity of situations that invoke the bully-victim attribution.

What learners do is associated with what they are permitted or expected to do. The rights of learners are usually explicit, because of their legal foundation, although they can be more problematic in practice than in principle. Learners' rights may be viewed as problematic if they are used to challenge institutional authority or to avoid responsibility for actions. With reference to learners' rights to participate in educational decisions, Harris (2009: 358) refers to the "hideous mass of complex legal and policy changes that continues to bedevil this area of the law". The chapter will outline roles that a learner might have and will then go on to examine their rights. The responsibilities of learners will be considered. Some of the tensions and inequalities that emerge will conclude the chapter.

Roles

Active-passive

It is important to qualify this continuum. *Passive* can be taken to mean simply the opposite of active—for instance, doing very little—although the origin of the word *passive* is *passivus*, Latin for 'being acted on'. Nowadays, *passive* can imply that someone is inactive in the acquiescent sense. Whether those who take a more passive role agree or have no choice in their positioning has implications for autonomy-dependence and for compliance-resistance. In this section, the term is used to refer to learners who have less involvement than teachers expect and thus experience educational processes as acting upon them rather than something they contribute to actively.

Taking an active role in one's learning and in the microcosm of institutions is often assumed; the 'best', most effective learners get involved in some way (see, e.g., Hattie, 2009). Little and Williams (2010: 116) assert that "students have always been expected to play an active role in the educational process". They are referring to higher education, but the same holds true for other learning places. For instance, Education Scotland's webpage (2014) on the roles and responsibilities of learners states that they "engage actively in learning".

There are a number of what might be described as more active, formal roles that learners can choose, or be chosen to take, within an institution. These include class representative, class monitor, school council member, head girl or boy, buddy, mentor and student union representative (see, e.g., Scottish Executive, 2006a; Welsh government, 2011b; NUS, 2008). Even very young learners can be involved. One Ofsted report (2007) praises the contribution of children aged three to seven to institutional matters in an English school.

More informal, and often self-appointed, roles can become apparent within classes or during group learning. A study of music students playing in quarters revealed a variety of roles: "leader, deputy-leader, contributor, inquirer, fidget, joker, distractor and 'quiet one'" (King, 2006: 262). In this small-scale study, having stable roles, and in particular being a consistent leader, was found to be more productive. Maloney's (2007) study of primary school children discussing science revealed both positive roles (such as chair or influential contributor) and negative ones (such as those involving reticence or distraction). The latter had a negative effect on argumentation and thus on group performance.

Teachers may assign a role such as monitor or class representative to a learner, or at least be instrumental in particular students ending up with a role. Some roles are described but not necessarily shared with learners, which does not mean that students are unaware of their label. Gallagher and Smith (2000) report that some grammar school teachers in Northern Ireland use the term *coasters* to refer to students who had been successful in securing a place but did little work thereafter. Other learners might be given the label *disappointers* if they were perceived to have been coached to gain a grammar school place but could not keep up once accepted. It is tempting for teachers to use labels to describe students. At best it serves no useful purpose, and at worst it may lead to a self-fulfilling prophecy, particularly problematic for the lower achievers who often attract more pejorative labels. Brophy (1982) reviewed the validity of the idea that treating learners according to expectations of achievement leads to expected outcomes. Although he concluded that context and mediating factors can influence whether labelling does in fact affect outcomes, his recommendations include concentrating on whole-class teaching more than individual differences and using individual, formative feedback without reference to normative outcomes. In attempts to 'differentiate', many inexperienced teachers I have observed believe they should either not ask reluctant students or underachievers questions at all or only ask question they think are simple enough to answer. This, I would say, is misplaced kindness, which positions certain students in a passive role and carries the risk of reducing achievement and resilience further, a phenomenon that is not restricted to the United Kingdom. One study in Taiwan reports a study found that teachers tended not to ask girls difficult questions because they were concerned about upsetting them (Hsieh, 2012).

Although teachers may plan activities for learners that will 'engage' them, it is often the case that learners spend much time listening, either to the teacher or to other learners. Watkins et al. (2007: 70) cite a survey that found most time in secondary schools was spent copying from the board and listening to "a teacher talking for a long time". Although the data were collected in 2004, my observations of teaching in further education indicate that many students are doing the same today, in spite of rhetoric that espouses student-centred learning. Learning could well involve listening and copying, but very often the justification for a particular teaching strategy is unclear or based on observation of or advice from other teachers, resulting in more passive than active learners. Osler and Flack realised the effect of their expectations on learners in a primary school context:

> [Passive behaviours] were so familiar to us as teachers that we found, at first, that we didn't see them as universal or unexpected, but we now see that they inadvertently lead students to develop poor learning tendencies. (2008: 3)

A study of secondary school used cartoons to illustrate (a) an objectivist approach (where teachers transmit information and learners remember it) and (b) a constructivist approach (where teachers find out what the learners know and engage in dialogue about learning). The analysis revealed a marked preference for (b), where learners play a more active role. Some staff in the schools selected expressed surprise at the results because "students had seemed so comfortable" (Kinchin, 2004: 305) with (a), which was the main teaching method.

Carol Dweck (1999) has written about learned helplessness, a response that works against the mastery approach to learning that she favours. The helpless learners in the research reported tended to give up in the face of difficulty and to attribute failure to lack of ability and that included high achievers. Learners who have learning rather than performance goals (such as a qualification), or who are encouraged to think in that way, tend to be more mastery oriented. In many institutions the emphasis is on summative assessment and grading to demonstrate the quality of education or to serve as a motivator, which is likely to encourage performance goals above learning that is founded on learners being active in overcoming challenge and becoming more proficient.

In addition to learning subjects, learners are usually expected to gain knowledge and skills that will support their active roles in education and in life more generally, including working life. This is true in schools, colleges, universities, prisons and some adult education. It may be explicitly stated as the purpose of education. The Scottish school curriculum aims to develop these four capacities: successful learners, confident individuals, responsible citizens and effective contributors (Education Scotland, website). For young people in particular, the lack of jobs and the extended period of compulsory education place additional pressure on education services to develop socially desirable attributes for a future that is very uncertain for many.

Autonomous-Dependent

Autonomy can either refer to acting independently of others or acting with power and authority, the first of which has been called local and the second global autonomy (Oshana, 2006). Both of these are relevant to the discussion here. Child development is marked by increasing autonomy, which, at least in Western cultures, has been identified by resistance and the demand for control (see, e.g., Woodhead, 1999). Young children's desire to be able to do things for themselves, whether by quiet imitation or through assertion, might indicate that learner autonomy could be expected; yet the demand for learners, particularly in further and higher education, to take more responsibility, as well as complaints from teachers about the spoon-feeding of students, indicates that autonomy has been eroded in some way but is highly valued by institutions. Some would argue that learner autonomy is "an essential goal of all learning" (Cotterall, 2000: 109). One report notes that:

> students actually became weaker as learners, especially in one key area—creativity. At the same time they became more dependent on teachers and others to help them learn, and less able to cope with mistakes and failure. (University of Bristol, 2003)

Subsequently, Guy Claxton and colleagues have formulated strategies that institutions can apply to combat the reduction in autonomy (see, e.g., Claxton et al., 2011).

John Webber and I investigated the notion of effective learners in a further education college. The findings of our small-scale study indicated that students on vocational courses were more dependent on teachers than those on more traditional A-level ones (McQueen & Webber, 2013). It could be that students on these courses have been positioned differently by prior institutions to behave in a more dependent way, a transactional effect that could be explained by different habitus (Bourdieu & Passeron, 1977) when the structured dispositions of a student interact with those of a teacher. Pastoral tutors were implicated, too, in our research because they could agree to extensions or offer other apparently supportive strategies that ultimately led to the construction of less effective learners. Once the role of a dependent learner has been perceived or established, it becomes increasingly difficult to find ways to encourage autonomy without coming across as unsympathetic or unsupportive in the face of a student's difficulties. I also researched transition to higher education with colleagues, which indicated how perceptions of student dependence created frustration and unhelpful responses. It also revealed the boundaries that university lecturers are trying to draw when it comes to support and what they perceive their role to be. One older adult student described her experience:

> She sat in her room and she said I don't care whether you turn up for lectures, seminars, she said I've got my degree so I'm not bothered whether you turn up or not . . . you've got to read it yourself and if you don't grasp the concept of it from a textbook then you feel like you can't go to a tutor to explain it to you, because that's not what they're there for, so you're left muddling along with it. (McQueen et al., 2009: 32–33)

Autonomy is a fundamental principle at Summerhill, an English fee-paying school that is founded on democratic principles. The most recent Ofsted report indicates what learners do. "Pupils are free to choose whether or not they attend lessons. When not in lessons, pupils can be involved in whatever activity that captures their interest. These include making films, organising and performing in musical or dramatic events, and learning different languages. Physical activities include trampolining, skateboarding, riding bikes and climbing trees" (Ofsted, 2011: 4).

Compliant-Resistant

Non-compliance, particularly in schools, is problematic for teachers but can have severe consequences for learners, too, since it may lead to temporary or permanent exclusion, thereby reducing achievement. The compliant role is a normative expectation of learners. Learners are expected to attend, to support school policies such as wearing the correct uniform, to behave well in school and in the community, and to take an active part in learning. Compliance does not require agreement with policy or practice but merely that objections are put to one side. In further and higher education, it is expected there will be compliance with a range of policies, including attendance, punctuality, meeting deadlines, avoiding plagiarism, and so forth. Reasons for failing to meet expectations, which include learners' own expectations, are many and varied; they may include problems with bullying, boredom, underachievement, lack of support, and peer or teacher relationships as well as difficulties at home, poverty, drug use, illness and combining study with paid work. Disruptive behaviour may be a sign of difficulties such as underachievement but can exacerbate the difficulties that learners experience. Myhill (2002) notes that underachieving boys tend to be less compliant, calling out and talking to neighbours, for example. Jackson (2003) investigated boys' behaviour, suggesting that fear of failure and fear of being perceived as feminine leads to behaviour that leads to lower achievement. For example, masculinity requires doing well without effort. There are different ways to display masculinity, some of which are "approved and legitimated within the educational sphere" (Wright et al., 2000: 65).

Non-compliant behaviour or resistance is often viewed as dispositional rather than situational. However, the resistant role can be viewed as essential to an understanding of the context of education within society and offers the potential to respond by making improvements to policy.

> Resistance . . . redefines the causes and meaning of oppositional behavior by arguing that it has little to do with the logic of deviance, individual pathology, learned helplessness (and, of course, genetic explanations), and a great deal to do, though not exhaustively, with the logic of moral and political indignation. (Giroux, 2001: 107)

Given that teachers have legitimate authority in institutions, it is almost inevitable that learners will be placed in a subordinate role of some kind. An American study of legitimacy and co-operation with policy indicated that supporting the police—and thus complying—depended both on accepting them as a legitimate authority and on perceptions of fair treatment (Tyler & Fagan, 2008). A Scottish study found that excluded learners often felt that they had been treated unfairly, although some accepted that exclusion was deserved (Munn & Lloyd, 2005). This study indicated that exclusion was a result of both what the learners did and who they were perceived to be. One referred to himself as the class clown, while another suggested he was treated differently because of the area he came from.

Expert-Novice

Learners may be placed on a continuum between expert and novice in terms of knowledge and skills. According to Stobart (2014), expert learners apply appropriate strategies, which include remembering, analysing and self-monitoring. The more expert learners demonstrate a degree of autonomy and self-regulation. They are able to do this because they have practised. What they practise depends on them having the interest and thus the motivation to practise it. Examples of expert learners cited are Wolfgang Amadeus Mozart and David Beckham, both of whom started practising at a young age with the support of their fathers, who shared an interest in music and football respectively.

The role of someone with more knowledge in nurturing expert learners is important if not imperative. According to Sennett (2008) that person is a master craftsman who provides the standards and appropriate training for the apprentice; the role of the apprentice is to practise, and the figure of approximately ten thousand hours is referred to. Similarly, Ericsson et al. (1993) emphasise deliberate practice for expertise in music performance above talent. Kalyuga et al. (2003) reviewed literature on instructions and guidance and found that these need to be geared to the level of the learner to be effective. Detailed guidance, for instance, can be unhelpful to more experienced learners who must process the information nonetheless, which gets in the way of processing the task. Conversely, those who are at a lower level are impeded by processing complex information, and they need more guidance to do so.

Learner-Teacher

The role of the expert can be much more subtle than telling someone what something is or how to do something. Indeed, it may not be essential to learning to have a teacher, or at least a person with that title, at all. Constructivists emphasise the building of knowledge and skills from the environment. An institutional environment contains a wealth of information that contributes to learning, including other learners who may take the role of teachers. When learners learn from each other, the term *peer tutor* tends to be used rather than *teacher*, presumably because the word *teacher* implies someone who has professional training or has been formally appointed to the role. Co-operative, peer-supported learning is founded on constructivist principles, and therefore experience and discovery learning, in which other learners offer intellectual conflict and challenge. Cognitive and social benefits of taking the learner-as-teacher approach have been reported (see, e.g., Topping, 2005). More radical social consequences of altering the teacher-learner hierarchy include greater autonomy and empowerment, which are central to Paolo Freire's (1970) vision for a less oppressive education system.

Academic-Vocational

This continuum, as indeed they all are, is infused with race, gender and class. Certain disciplines or subjects, which may be designated as academic and vocational, are unequally represented by different social groups. There is a strong association between wider social roles and being, or rather becoming, an 'academic' or 'vocational' learner. The concept of habitus is useful because it is part of what makes a subject or type of learning preferable. Colley et al. (2004: 488) use the term *vocational habitus*, by which they mean "a process of orientation to a particular identity, a sense of what makes 'the right person for the job'." Therefore what the learner does is important in constructing a notion of the type of learner someone is and thus whether he or she is more suited to the academic or vocational route that education has been rather unhelpfully divided into. Ingle and Duckworth (2013) propose that vocational education is geared towards a job, or at least more obviously so. More crudely, the distinction is often made between doers (vocational) and thinkers (academic) or between lower achievers (vocational) and higher achievers (academic). Perceptions of who students 'are' become important when choices between subjects and institutions or between employment and continuing education need to be made because there is evidence that teachers are influential in decision making about appropriate courses to take (Blenkinsop et al., 2006).

Past-Future Roles

Negotiating the education system invokes notions of where 'a person like me' might be going. Ball et al. (2000: 51) refer to 'imagined futures' and the part these play in making educational choices.

> For some their imagined futures are relatively clear, relatively stable and relatively possible. For a second group their imagined future is vague, relatively unstable and beset with uncertainties. A third group has at this stage no imagined future which can provide a focus or locus for decision making.

Learners of all ages are prone to the influence of others—parents, teachers, peers, siblings, friends, employers, and media figures—with habitus shaping whose influence is stronger or more stable.

There have been a number of studies investigating the futures that people think about in relation to education, such as whether to choose an academic or vocational subject, whether to attend a particular institution, or whether to continue with formal education at all. Markus and Nurius (1987: 157) introduced the term *possible selves* to refer to "individuals' ideas of what they might become, what they would like to become, and what they are afraid of becoming".

The possibilities for the future depend on past experiences yet also contribute to how experiences are perceived. Consequently, possible selves influence "goals, aspirations, motives, fears, and threats" (ibid.: 158). Given that much education is founded on the notion of progression and preparation for the future, the effect of possible selves can be highly influential. For example, Stevenson and Clegg (2011) found that there was a difference between students regarding their ability to look to the future or to develop themselves for employability. Working-class students' extracurricular activity was more likely to be paid work, whereas middle-class students were more likely to take part in sport or music activities. Creech et al. (2014) consider the value of possible selves arising from music activities for older adults as a means to enhance a sense of well-being in later life.

Bully-Victim

These roles are important in relation to learning because some of those who are bullied tend to achieve less and are more likely to end up not in education, employment or training (NEET) (Equality and Human Rights Commission, 2010). Bullying is associated with asserting dominance over another and engaging in some form of aggression as part of that assertion (Lines, 2008). Those defined as bullies are at risk of temporary or permanent exclusion, whereas victims may exclude themselves by increased absence. Victims may suffer permanent psychological harm from bullying experiences. Some social groups are more prone to bullying than others, although individual victims may be selected because they lack self-esteem or appear to be different physically or in character to the norm. For example, Lundy (2007) reports higher bullying rates for Travellers in Northern Ireland. Data from other UK regions indicate that disability, minority ethnicity, and, in particular, sexual orientation influence the likelihood of being bullied.

One assumption that might be made is that the bully does more than the victim, or in other words, bullying behaviour is active whereas being a victim is passive. Although that might appear to be the case, victim behaviour is often more complex, and it is not simply a case of being on the receiving end of another's aggression. Passive and provocative victims, as well as bully-victims who have experience of both roles, are described in Juvonen and Graham's book (2001). In addition, the relational aspects that Lines (2008) refers to are significant because institutional context is important and because it is rarely a matter of two individuals in conflict. Salmivalli (1999) refers to bullying as a group phenomenon in which a number of individuals take different roles such as assistant or encourager of the bully. There are no doubt many instances when bullying is circumvented by the co-operative or peace-making roles of individuals in a group, but they are likely to be unreported, unnoticed or unrecognised.

Rights

Stewart et al. (2007: 3) state that rights "may be categorised into welfare and liberty rights or, as more commonly stated in relation to children, protection and participation rights". The right to participate is tempered by the belief that children do not have the experience and broader understanding required to make rational decisions about what they should do. Although learners at all levels could be described as consumers and stakeholders, their power is unequal to that of other stakeholders (Evans & Gill, 2001).

Right to an Education

The right to an education is a fundamental principle in the United Kingdom, which is a signatory to the rights outlined by the United Nations. Article 26 of the Universal Declaration of Human Rights (United Nations, 1948) states:

1. Everyone has the right to education. Education shall be free, at least in the elementary and fundamental stages. Elementary education shall be compulsory. Technical and professional education shall be made generally available and higher education shall be equally accessible to all on the basis of merit.
2. Education shall be directed to the full development of the human personality and to the strengthening of respect for

human rights and fundamental freedoms. It shall promote understanding, tolerance and friendship among all nations, racial or religious groups, and shall further the activities of the United Nations for the maintenance of peace.
3. Parents have a prior right to choose the kind of education that shall be given to their children.

Further to this declaration, the United Kingdom signed the United Nations Convention on the Rights of the Child (CRC) in 1990, and the convention became law in 1992 (Department for Education, 2014b). Of the 193 countries that are members of the United Nations, only the United States and Somalia have not signed the Convention on the Rights of the Child (UNICEF and United Nations websites). *Child* refers to anyone under the age of 18, unless there is a different age of majority in a particular country. The age of majority is 18 in Wales, England and Northern Ireland but 16 in Scotland. The convention lays out rights to care, protection and education with the ideal of an upbringing "in the spirit of peace, dignity, tolerance, freedom, equality and solidarity" (UNICEF, 1989: 3). The following articles are pertinent to learners:

- Articles 12 and 13—freedom of expression, although the weight of views depends on age and maturity and the right might be restricted by law or in order to protect others.
- Article 14—freedom of thought, conscience and religion, although parental rights are granted that may counter children's rights.
- Article 23—recognition of the right to a "full and decent life" (ibid.: 8) for mentally or physically disabled children, including access to education and training.
- Article 28—a right to free, compulsory primary education with the hope that secondary education will be available, too. This secondary education should "include general and vocational education" (ibid.: 9). States should encourage attendance and aim to reduce dropout rates. Discipline should be "consistent with the child's human dignity". The final point avers that there should be international cooperation with regard to education, "in particular with a view to contributing to the elimination

of ignorance and illiteracy throughout the world" as well as opportunities to gain "scientific and technical knowledge and modern teaching methods".
- Article 29—education should develop the "child's personality, talents and mental and physical abilities to their fullest potential". Education should also develop respect for others and the natural environment so that a child is prepared for "responsible life in a free society".
- Article 30—the right to enjoy the culture of one's family's indigenous origin, including religion and language.
- Article 31—the right to embrace "cultural, artistic, recreational and leisure activity" (ibid.: 10).

Right to Complain or Appeal

Pupils in schools in the United Kingdom have a right to complain about a perceived injustice. In England this right was set out in the Apprenticeship, Skills, Children and Learning Act (2009). Other regions base the right on the CRC. In practice, owing to power differentials, school ethos and the lack of a system through which student complaints may be channelled, parents may well be the ones to complain on behalf of their children.

A remarkable court case demonstrated the value of young people's right to appeal. The views of pupils—specifically that they have the right to choose the kind of education they receive—formed part of the court case that arose from a 1999 Ofsted inspection of Summerhill that severely criticised the school. The school won the case and now has an inspection that is specific to the ethos of the school (Summerhill website).

Students have the right to appeal against a judgement of their achievement, particularly external exams. Schools or colleges may submit an enquiry if the results do not seem correct. Appeals may lead to marks going down. Checking for clerical errors, asking to have a paper returned to see the marking, and asking for a re-mark have become increasingly common but remain relatively infrequent compared with the total number of awards. For instance, Ofqual (2013) reports that for the summer 2012 exam series, close to six million GCSE results were issued in England, Wales and Northern Ireland. That year there were almost 280,000 enquiries in relation to over 21 million unit entries. Approximately 0.5 per cent of results were altered. No national data are available for the number of appeals or complaints made by higher education students. All universities offer students the right to appeal, and individual complaints may be addressed to the Office of the Independent Adjudicator for England and Wales, the board of visitors in Northern Ireland and the Scottish Public Services Ombudsman as part of the Model Complaints Handling Procedure in Scotland. Students may complain if they were insufficiently protected from psychological or physical harm. Evans and Gill (2001) report court cases where this has been the cause for complaint. The legal aspect involved means that complaints tend to be dealt with on a case-by-case basis and do not address institutional practice directly or at least openly.

Right to Participate

The right to express opinions and to be a democratic partner in education is touched on in the human rights documents introduced above. There is reference in government policy and institutional documents to involving learners in decisions about education, which may include what and how they are taught. Summerhill has been referred to as an institution that is founded on democratic principles. Other institutions draw on democratic principles although there is variation in practice.

> Pupils *are* observant and have a rich but often untapped understanding of processes and events; ironically, they often use their insights to devise strategies for avoiding learning, a practice which, over time, can be destructive of their progress. (Rudduck & Flutter, 2000: 83)

Participation may be through school councils or consultation during inspections. Learners in further and higher education can be represented by the National Union of Students and by "student participation in quality Scotland" (sparqs).

The rights of those with special educational needs (SEN) to participate are acknowledged in policy and rhetoric but require attention if they are to be meaningfully upheld. Some institutions have found innovative ways to increase participation that does not rely on learners talking (Norwich, 2013). It was pointed out that learners' rights are moderated by beliefs about cognitive competence. As Brahm Norwich says, however, the barriers identified were not entirely agreed upon by adults and children with SEN. There was agreement that children can be unwilling to participate and that participation depends on trustful relationships. Adults thought children were not necessarily capable of participating, while children identified concerns about confidentiality, unapproachability of adults, tokenism, slow positive responses and lack of control over the use of their views.

Responsibilities

Concern that learners are not taking responsibility for their learning or lack autonomy or independence has been expressed by governments, teachers and the media (see, e.g., Scottish government, 2010; Meyer et al., 2008). It might be apparent from the outline of roles and rights above that the education system can mitigate a sense of responsibility. Little (1995) suggests that formal educational contexts tend to reduce responsibility unless teachers find strategies to combat the effect. Learner outcomes are an important part of institutional performance, but driving up achievement often leads to more didactic, teaching-to-the-test methods, which reduces opportunities for learner autonomy. Therefore responsibility, autonomy, independence, or their opposites can refer to roles taken by learners in response to the context in which they find themselves learning.

Exhortations for learners to be more responsible are rarely effective, and it is often the teacher who is held accountable for poor outcomes. It may be that a better word here would be *duty*. The role of the learner carries implicit duties, such as making an effort or 'actively engaging' as some might say. Duties of learners, whether explicit or implicit, might include acting autonomously. Even if that were confined to matters of learning, it would mean that choosing to opt out of certain aspects of education could be perfectly reasonable, even if that choice led to reduced achievement in one or more areas; such choices would be resisted within an accountable system, however. The issue of responsibility is a site of tension and is considered further in the next section.

Tensions

Autonomy-Dependence

A theme that has run through this chapter is that of how the education system works to encourage or discourage learner independence. The onus that has been placed on institutions to be accountable for learner outcomes has created a tension for teachers who may like to work in less restricted ways but find themselves trapped into practice that limits learning to what the teacher decides should be learnt or what needs to be known for exams. The tension arises from a state of affairs in education where learners and teachers are caught between a more conservative, traditional, instruction-led and a more progressive, student-centred approach to education. The former is characterised by compliance and the latter by self-regulation (Jonassen & Land, 2000). Learners are sometimes expected to be compliant, passive and dependent but at other times to be active, responsible and thus autonomous. Furthermore, particular forms of compliance and autonomy are viewed as appropriate within the confines of institutional authority.

The tendency for teachers to limit learner autonomy, often inadvertently, has been recognised. Whitebread et al. (2005) used mixed methods to study and support teachers of children aged three to five in relation to self-regulated learning. Over time, teachers encouraged rather than praised, suggested another child could help rather than the teacher, and intervened less in disputes. When children were permitted to make choices and decisions, they were organised and motivated. A study conducted with further education students that looked into notions of independent learning indicated that taking responsibility for learning is important, classrooms are not conducive to autonomy and vocational students had fewer opportunities for independent learning (Broad, 2006). Vocational students are often required to produce coursework, and they become dependent on feedback from teachers to make improvements. These and other studies emphasise the role of the teacher in providing opportunities to work more independently in a constructive way and without resorting to coercive or therapeutic strategies (see, e.g., Ecclestone and Hayes's critique of therapeutic education, 2009). A more nuanced understanding of what 'support' constitutes is needed if learners are to take a more autonomous role.

Learner Comfort or Risk and Challenge

The dilemma here arises from concerns about how to balance the daily lives and emotional needs of learners with the discomfort that is an integral part of learning. An expression that one hears a great deal is *comfort zone*, defined by White (2008: 2) as follows:

> The comfort zone is a behavioural state within which a person operates in an anxiety-neutral condition, using a limited set of behaviours to deliver a steady level of performance, usually without a sense of risk.

As White points out, the steady level of performance can mitigate learning and progression. Many psychological theories espouse the notion of a degree of challenge for the purpose of learning. These include disequilibrium and optimal arousal. Piaget (1936) proposed that learning resulted from a mismatch between what is known and new information that creates cognitive challenge or disequilibrium. Cognitive development arises when mental structures (schemata) change to allow for new information. Optimal arousal (Hebb, 1955) refers to a midpoint between over arousal and under arousal that facilitates actions such as problem solving. Some anxiety or at least a sense of disconcertment is essential to learning.

Each year in the United Kingdom a university student survey is conducted which measures satisfaction. The latest statistics indicate satisfaction is high (HEFCE, 2013). Of course knowing that satisfaction is to be measured in a consistent fashion can lead to 'working to the test' by attending to those items known to be measured. Furthermore, statistical data based on ratings of satisfaction neither explain the source of satisfaction nor its relevance to learning. A considerable number of students are not satisfied according to the data, although the source of the dissatisfaction is unclear. Furedi (2011: 4) challenges the principle of student satisfaction:

> From a Socratic perspective the very term 'student satisfaction' is an irrational one. Why? Because students need to be placed under intellectual pressure, challenged to experience the intensity of problem solving.

It should be acknowledged that what constitutes intellectual pressure at any stage in the education system depends upon a range of factors. There could be an assumption that the intellectual challenge involved is in working with the particular ideas or problems. However, many students are challenged by the form that information is presented in. Bernstein (1961) distinguished between public and formal communication; with the reading of books on the decline, the increase in multilingualism, and text-speak pervading written formats, a new set of challenges have arisen around shared forms of communication.

Humanistic psychology has been influential in raising awareness of the emotional needs of learners as part of a more holistic approach to learning. Carl Rogers was a leading proponent of humanism in education who was concerned about the adherence to conventional methods that include teachers lecturing "to death" (1983: 15). "We have paid our taxpayers' money in order to have our children scarred, damaged, hurt, and stultified—changed from eager learners into active rebels against education" (107). The therapeutic element already referred to is a by-product of attention to the social and emotional aspects of learning. Important though these may be, they can lead to a diminished view of learners' capabilities and desires, the very opposite of humanistic notions of personal growth and responsible freedom. For example, research into activities for older learners revealed some of the activity leaders placed comfort above challenge. In a paper derived from the research (McQueen et al., 2013), we concluded thus: as Ecclestone and Hayes (2009: 84) argue, "[t]he danger in exercises that 'facilitate' and assess self-esteem and confidence is that they elevate these commonplace by-products of good teaching into central goals of learning, creating a desire to 'ease' and 'smooth' discomfort and to avoid challenge and risk". Rogers pointed out himself that the problem of implementing an alternative kind of provision is that teachers rarely have appropriate knowledge of how to do it well. The demand for student-centred education can turn a liberating education on its head. "Anything can become an imposed rule, even freedom" (Rogers, 1983: 247).

Consumerism in Education

Related to learner satisfaction and to active and passive roles is the tension regarding the role of the learner as consumer, a "dominant metaphor for the student" (Nordensvärd, 2011). More has been written about consumerism in higher education, although it is relevant to school choice and to post-compulsory education. The role of consumer may be at odds with the idea of the learner as a developing agent with broadening and deepening understanding of a topic or field of study. Furedi (2011) is not against competition between institutions but points out the potential for a different kind of educational experience, one that provides the type of education that learners think they want rather than one that might be educationally desirable. However, as he points out, this is a long-standing problem rather than a new development.

Molesworth et al. (2009) say that learners have been placed in the position of consumers by the marketization of education and by the role of universities in supporting economic growth. They distinguish between the 'having mode' (getting a degree, for instance) and the 'being mode'. The latter allows for focus on achievement—a learning goal rather than a performance one. The distinction was made originally by Erich Fromm (1976, 2007), who separates a way of living that is based on possession (having) from one that is more authentic (being). Those in the being mode are not "passive receptacles of words and ideas" but "*respond* in an active, productive way" (25).

Inequalities

Access and Participation

There is no doubt that some form of education is available for all, a marked improvement on the state of affairs prior to the 1944 Butler Act. The right to an education could be said to have been fulfilled. The CRC does not specify what is meant by *education* aside from promoting values such as freedom and greater tolerance. In spite of government policy that upholds the right to an education, there remains unequal access to some types of education, notably those that are fee paying or selective.

In order to access education, either learners need to attend an institution or there has to be alternative provision. Home schooling is not an option for the majority (see chapter 4). Private tutoring is too costly for most families. There are distance learning opportunities for a range of courses, including qualifications that are more often gained at school, college or university; these opportunities depend on possessing independent learning skills and on being able to afford them.

Access to education for prisoners varies, with security issues hampering opportunities. Education, training and skill development are particularly important for those in prison because so many have few or no qualifications. The majority of prisoners are men; in England and Wales, a quarter are from an ethnic minority group, and 13 per cent are Muslim (but only 4 per cent in the population) (Berman & Dar, 2013). A longitudinal survey of 1,435 prisoners indicated that they tended to have disrupted childhoods and had played truant; 47 per cent had no academic qualifications. Being in prison offers an opportunity to access education, but some areas and methods of study are restricted or prohibited—for instance, science education, use of the Internet, and vocational training that could pose a security risk (Hurry et al., 2012).

Although education may be available and accessible, not everyone participates. While some choose not to attend and are truants, others are temporarily or permanently excluded. The United Nations Committee on the Rights of the Child (2008) was concerned by the number of ethnic minority children excluded from schools, thereby depriving them of their right to an education. Boys are more likely to be permanently excluded. Non-attendance is more likely among travelling communities, children in custody or immigration detention and children of asylum seekers (Equality and Human Rights Commission [EHRC], 2010). Although life may not be entirely fair, there is unequal experience of unfairness. Young people in a Scottish study "readily distinguished occasions when they brought exclusion upon themselves, and accepted responsibility for this, from occasions when they saw exclusion as an unfair or unreasonable reaction [of staff] to a particular set of circumstances" (Munn & Lloyd, 2005: 208). Problems leading to exclusion are more to do with the relations between staff and young people or between young people than with individuals rebelling against a system (Wright et al., 2000).

The right to participate could be interpreted in a number of ways. Shier (2001) refers to five levels of participation: children are listened to, supported in expressing their views, have those views taken into account, are involved with decision making and "share power and responsibility for decision-making" (110). In schools, opportunities to participate in these ways vary. Participation offered through school councils or consultation during inspections offers the possibility for learners to be listened to and supported in expressing their views. Other levels of participation are unlikely, particularly sharing of power. The unequal weight given to adults' and children's views can be justified by the suggestion that adults are acting in children's best interests and that they know best, although neither assertion is necessarily correct. Although encouraging participation can be problematic, those identified by Lansdown (2001) are not restricted to children; rather they are part of negotiation processes in a plethora of situations. Problems include unequal representation of a group, representatives that become separated from those they represent, short-term participation and manipulation by an agenda.

Educational Development

According to the EHRC (2010), there are marked differences by the age of five. Girls, regardless of ethnicity, have on average more advanced social, emotional, and cognitive development with the greatest difference being in writing. Those eligible for free school meals, an indicator of low income, are at a disadvantage, as are black and Pakistani children. The advantage that girls have over boys at age 5 continues to age 16. Although differences in achievement have narrowed between ethnic groups, some remain ahead and others behind in achievement; Indian and Chinese children have an advantage, Travellers and Gypsy or Roma a disadvantage. Young people from poorer backgrounds do worse (ibid.).

Being taught by cover (from within the school) or supply (brought in from outside) teachers can impede progress. For example, a report by Estyn (2013) indicates that behaviour and achievement are worse in classes that are taught by supply teachers, particularly in secondary schools. Supply teachers may not be subject specialists and do not know the learners well. Teacher absence is inevitable, but analysis of whether some schools, and consequently particular learners, are affected more than others would be instructive.

Access to education in prisons can be problematic, but so too can development. There are a number of organisational challenges in relation to educational development, particularly for prisoners who move to a different prison or who are released during a course of study (Hurry et al., 2012). Inequalities in access to and progression in education for the prison population can therefore compound the disadvantage experienced by those already disadvantaged from a young age.

There are clear trends in inequality, with implications for the kind of life that certain members of society are likely to have. Autonomy and responsibility are promoted as valuable attributes but often on the assumption that individuals are free agents who could choose to overcome hurdles and barriers set up by inequalities. Institutional policy recognises some of these obstacles and may have partial success in changing outcomes for some. However, although institutions can contribute to combating some of the factors that impede progress, they can be seen as both pathogen and remedy. For this reason they often have limited scope to bring about "fundamental transformations" (Kerr & West, 2010: 8).

Educational Pathways and Choice

Education consists of a number of forced or restricted choices for the majority. For some there may be more choice, depending on the amount of social or economic capital available. Where someone lives is an important factor, with those living in remote or rural areas usually having reduced choice. It is inevitable that not all pathways will be available to all, however desirable. Inequality derives from a system that channels people down a particular pathway from an early age. The main division is between vocational and academic education. There are various reasons why particular choices are made either by learners themselves or with encouragement or guidance from parents, teachers or personal tutors. Reasons include enjoyment or intrinsic interest, higher achievement or ease of learning, a clear pathway to a job or career, and tradition (part of academic or vocational habitus). Most institutions strive to raise achievement, and one way is to allocate learners according to perceived potential for achievement. Of course the allocation might be justified as a means to help people to succeed, which is a form of coercive paternalism or interference (Conly, 2013). Teachers, parents, or other advisers know better what a person is suited to than the person.

Cook (2013: 13) writes:

> In all of the research reviewed that sought the views of teachers and head teachers it was apparent that vocational qualifications were seen as beneficial for those who were disengaged from schools and/or low attainers.

Those who do well in academic subjects may be put off taking them because they are assigned a lower status. Cook, with reference to England, suggests that improvements to the system could include improving the vocational education that is offered and adjusting performance measures that emphasise academic attainment above vocational. However, altering the value of subjects of qualifications is unlikely to be achieved because they reflect wider inequalities in society and entrenched ideologies. Inequality of credentials and life chances (Tyler, 2012 [1977]) look set to remain.

Tyler (ibid.: 131) concludes his book on the sociology of educational inequality thus:

> Despite the huge amount of public money that the educational system eats up, the mechanism of selection, allocation and rewards is still not working according to any model of social engineering and probably never will . . . If educational inequality is to be cured we must get beyond both individualism and rhetoric and look at those structures and processes of industrial societies which do not necessarily follow the logic of one's world view. Only when this is done will it be possible to distinguish between those inequalities that are indispensable to productivity and liberty and those historic abuses which could well be swept away.

Who might be the ones, the 'we', to take up this challenge is not at all clear. Today's learners might be the very people to take on the role and to reconsider their worldview in order to uphold more equal rights and life chances.

Chapter Summary

In this chapter some of the dilemmas, tensions and inequalities with regard to learners are explored. John Webber, in his preface, describes ways in which one college of further education in England is working to maintain quality whilst resisting the tendency to produce or to maintain learners who are passive and dependent. The section on roles is an analysis of what learners do, structured according to a number of dichotomies. These are active-passive, autonomous-dependent, compliant-resistant, expert-novice, learner-teacher, academic-vocational, past-future, and bully-victim. The socially constructed nature of roles is referred to, with implications for both teachers and parents in shaping the experience of education and subsequent outcomes. Learners' rights have a basis in law through acceptance of the Convention on the Rights of the Child. Rights to an education, to participate and to complain are discussed. What learners are responsible for is questioned and included as a source of tension. Other tensions relate to autonomy-dependence, comfort-challenge and consumerism. Inequalities selected for this chapter include differences between learners in the extent to which they have access to different forms of education and the degree to which they can participate. The final inequality is that of unequal educational development, which can depend on characteristics of learners, such as gender and cultural background, as well as institutional impediments to progress.

CHAPTER 4

Parents

Parents, Gender and Education

Miriam E. David, Emeritus Professor, Institute of Education, London

This chapter is a snapshot of current thinking about 'parents'. Questions about home-school relations have for a long time taxed policy makers and social researchers. To understand better how the idea of 'parents' in relation to the ever-changing education 'system' has come about, we need knowledge of educational policy developments, their economic and social contexts, and the voluminous research into mothers' and fathers' involvements and investments in education; how parents' choices, roles and responsibilities are constrained by sexual and social expectations about who they are and what they should do; and, most importantly, what their sons and daughters should learn to be and do. I provide some historical evidence of policy changes and examples of research on mothers and fathers and social and sexual expectations today.

The State, The Family and Education (David, 1980) reviewed key developments for parents and the parallel changes in the teaching profession to analyse 'the family-education couple'. In summary, 150 years ago, there was no education 'system' as we know it today, and women as mothers, wives, daughters, and sisters were not educated on a par with men—fathers, husbands, sons and brothers—whatever their social, religious or cultural family backgrounds. Whilst there were 'dame' schools—run by single women or spinsters for young children, equivalent to nurseries and infant schools today—they were not funded by the state. It was only in 1870 that the state began to make schools available to the masses, and when made compulsory, parents still had to pay fees; as many could not afford to do so, their children did not routinely attend.

Over the next 70 years, schooling was extended for different classes of family, although boys were afforded better opportunities than girls, in the expectation that they would become the family 'breadwinners' and girls would become 'wives and mothers' staying at home to care for the family. Indeed a 'marriage bar' was imposed so that married women could not routinely work, particularly not as teachers. Towards the end of the Second World War, the framework for postwar education was set through the 1944 Education Act. A commitment to equality of educational opportunity aiming to equalise between children from family backgrounds of privilege and those in poverty or of working-class background or both was made. Although differences between boys and girls were not explicit, there were expectations that it was mothers' responsibility to make sure children were ready and able to benefit from education. Little state help with preschool children was provided, so mothers inevitably had to stay at home.

It was another 30 years before any modest provisions were made for state nursery education, and it is still the case that they are not funded as generously as compulsory education. It was not until the 1960s that women teachers got equal pay on a par with men, given the ongoing assumption that men were the breadwinners and women the stay-at-home mothers; other workers did not get equal pay until after the 1975 Equal Pay Act! For 44 years there was a bipartisan political consensus on equality of opportunity, but the Education

> Reform Act (ERA) transformed this to markets and parental choice in education.
>
> In *Parents, Gender and Education Reform* (1993), using Brown's concept of parentocracy, changing expectations for mothers to invest in their children's education were explored. The realities of mothering and schooling were looked at in *Mothers and Education: Inside Out?* (David et al., 1993), in which case studies showed the constraints on mothers' other work, given their responsibilities for bringing up children. *Mother's Intuition? Choosing Secondary Schools* (David et al., 1994) showed how it was mothers who did the legwork of looking for appropriate schools, with fathers merely ratifying their decisions. *Get Real About Sex: The Politics and Practice of Sex Education* (Alldred & David, 2007) explored how schools and parents today think about healthy sexual relationships and where they should be taught, either at home or at school, for boys and girls to learn to be the mothers and fathers of the future. In *What Should We Tell Our Daughters?*, Benn (2013) reviews the evidence accumulated from research showing how changing social expectations still need to be contested for future generations of mothers and fathers.

The term *parent* in policy documents and in general speech inadequately captures the various types of parents and forms of parenting that exist. For example, when 'parental involvement' is referred to, does this mean one parent or two, and if two, do they have equal involvement? No doubt many people will think of the biological mother or father as a parent. However, a parent can be anyone who cares for or who has responsibility for a child until the child reaches the age of majority. They include single parents, two men, two women, foster parents, adoptive parents, grandparents or other relatives. In this chapter the word *parent* could refer to any of the possible definitions. However, it is important to be mindful of the normative assumptions that can be attached to the word *parent* when reading this chapter and to consider how relevant each aspect might be to each person who falls under the category of *parent*. Such assumptions might include an upbringing by two parents, one male and one female or the parent being a biological one.

One often hears more *about* parents than one does *from* them in UK education policy and research. What research there is tends to be focused on specific groups or educational issues, including class, race, and special educational needs (see, e.g., Vincent et al. 2012; Paradice and Adewusi, 2002). One text that reports a range of research into parental involvement, which is more often that of mothers, is *Activating Participation* (Crozier & Reay, 2005); yet now, as then, parents are not "democratically participative" (ibid.: x). Ofsted has an online survey for parents at the time of writing (Parent View, 2013), although it is restricted to twelve questions relating to views about their child's school rather than the education system in general. Indeed, Jacky Lumby (2007) suggested that parents' views are considered to be less relevant than teachers', and no doubt those of other education 'experts', because ostensibly they are influenced by a narrow focus on what would be best for their child rather than the greater good. Such an attitude reflects an individualistic and competitive society, one which fails to consider the deleterious effects that individual success can have on the society that one is part of. In spite of a shift towards increased parental involvement in their child's education either through school choice, school creation, or home-school agreements and collaboration, parents, for the most part, have relatively little say in education policy. Their role as consumers of education is, for the majority, restricted by the educational diet on offer.

It is hard to challenge the suggestion that "all parents want the best for their children" (Sarah Teather, Children's Minister, Department for Education, 2012a). It is less difficult to question both how one defines 'the best' and the presumption that all parents can have what is deemed to be 'the best'. Little has changed in this respect. Alexander's guide for parents on the 1944 Butler Act assumes that parents will want to co-operate with the reforms and "throw their full weight behind the efforts of the local education authorities and of the Ministry" (1946: 37) because of the benefits to their children. This weight now seems to be thrown more directly behind young people by some parents. The terms *helicopter parenting* and *lawn mower parenting* have been in vogue recently, indicating a form of relative over-parenting (constantly hovering over one's children's affairs or clearing the pathway to success through intervention) that, whilst undoubtedly not a new phenomenon in the history of being a parent, is a strategic way to get ahead of the competition and to combat youthful disinterest or doubtful success. There are therefore cultural norms and expectations of a parent's role in education, which may in some cases start before birth (e.g., putting a child's name down for a private school or considering where to live to assist in securing a place at a preferred maintained school) and continue until education ceases, which may be at the postgraduate level.

In the first section of this chapter, the roles of parents in UK education are set out. The second section deals with parental rights. The main right is that of choice, or at least perceived choice, which has shifted more responsibility onto parents. The "vast subject" (Monk, 2009: 144) of parental responsibility will be explored in the third section. The final section of the chapter outlines some of the tensions and inequalities in relation to parents and UK education.

Roles

Only so much can be said about what parents do in terms of their children's education before one is confronted by what they are able to do, legally, morally, financially, and practically. Parental roles are also dependent on the child's age and the type of education (e.g., private or state). In this section, the following will be discussed in relation to parental roles:

- Choosing a place for education
- Preparing children for the education system
- Monitoring progress and behaviour
- Getting involved with education
- Supporting and challenging the education system

Choosing a Place for Education

Choosing a school has become increasingly important for many parents and is part of the shift from centralised systems to marketisation and privatisation (see, e.g., Whitty and Power, 2000). Parents are now "consumers of education" (Hughes et al., 1994: ix) who can use information provided by the school, such as exam results or attendance data, and the views of others (parents and their own children) to select an appropriate school. This increased power in deciding which schools are the chosen ones has been suggested as a third wave in education, parentocracy, the first two being mass schooling in the late nineteenth century and post-war meritocracy (Brown, 1994).

According to West (1994), location is important, particularly for the choice of primary school, whereas exam results, level of discipline and resources are some of the criteria for the choice of secondary school. The Millennium Cohort Study (Hansen et al., 2010), a longitudinal study of 19,000 children born in 2000–2001, found that a minority of parents opt for private (fee-paying) primary schools (5 per cent in England, 3 per cent in Northern Ireland and 2 per cent in Wales and Scotland). There was a highly significant association between this choice and mothers being educated to degree level. For the majority of parents, the choice is between state (government-maintained) schools. In Scotland parents are allocated a primary school, although they can apply for a different one. In the rest of the United Kingdom, parents are given a form to complete. The percentage of parents exercising choice was approximately 80 per cent in England, 60 per cent in Wales, 40 per cent in Scotland and 90 per cent in Ireland. The reasons given for making a choice were proximity of school, whether friends or siblings were there, school performance and other school characteristics. The first two reasons were more frequently given for choice of state school and the latter two for choice of private school.

Parents might also choose to home educate their children, although many parents might be unwilling or unable to do so. The non-normative choice to home educate might lead to the assumption that there is greater homogeneity of those making this choice than is the case, or at least this homogeneity is "superficial" (Rothermel 2002: 83). In Paula Rothermel's study of 419 families, the main reason for choosing to home educate was dissatisfaction with mainstream education closely followed by a long-standing intention and because of bullying at school. However, there were frequently multiple reasons. The role that parents have in choosing their children's education ties in with responsibility. Indeed, taking responsibility for their children's education was frequently referred to as a motivation (op. cit.). Nonetheless, conflicting roles (such as working and caring for others) make home education an impossible choice for many. Rothermel's concern is that if more families do choose to home educate, then UK governments will view the choice as "problematised" (op. cit.: 87) and will tighten up regulations, thereby limiting parental rights whilst increasing parental responsibility.

Preparing Children for an Education System

The home provides a 'developmental niche' (Super & Harkness, 1986) in which a child is prepared consciously or otherwise for his or her future. The process of preparing children for the education system will have started well before that first day at school, whether at nursery or primary or secondary school, although the role of parents is greater in preparation for early-years education since teachers are also involved in preparing children for secondary school. Some preparation takes place prenatally. The popular website Mumsnet is a source of information and guidance for parents, although its name suggests the main users will be mothers. The prenatal advice refers to health-related behaviour, including diet and drugs, with an emphasis on producing a healthy baby. The maternal environment is implicated in a child's behavioural, cognitive and social outcomes. Devlin et al. (1997) provide support for the significant role that the prenatal maternal environment has in intelligence, for example. There are books and websites available on teaching babies in utero and from birth. Reading or playing music to the unborn child are advocated, partly a result of the misapplied research on what is known as the Mozart effect (Rauscher et al., 1995). Postnatally, the use of sign language for hearing babies is being promoted to enhance communication, thereby reducing infants' frustrations, and to improve literacy (see, e.g., *Baby Signing Time!*). The point here is that popular media, which offer a mixture of common sense advice and selected research findings, are instrumental in emphasising the role that mothers in particular have in determining the future success of their child.

Postnatal parental roles in education include those involving choice and use of toys, supporting language and numeracy development, managing emotions, discussing ideas and so forth. According to Likierman and Muter (2006: 13), "the way you prepare your child for school is crucial". The suggestion that transitions are problematic is prevalent, and parents are implicated in easing the change from one situation to another for their child. One option might be to read an appropriate book such as *Starting School* (Ahlberg & Ahlberg, 1990) to, as the publishers say, "calm the anxieties and to encourage the enthusiasm of pre-school children" (Puffin Books online). Most UK universities offer advice to parents about how to apply (e.g., Oxford University) or how to keep in touch with their children and when to visit once accepted (e.g., University of Hertfordshire).

Preschool education is now the norm, although children are not legally required to attend school until their fifth year. Indeed, choosing a nursery school is at the top of the list in the 'Education' section of Mumsnet. Nursery schools, playgroups and child minders extend the developmental niche beyond the home. Although working parents need alternative child care, they can use that as part of the socialisation into school processes and circumstances. These include meeting other children, increasing independence and learning some basic elements of reading, writing and numeracy. One aim is to reduce the expected angst referred to above when children go to school, particularly through the choice of nursery schools. In a small-scale study of Scottish working-class parents, Caddell et al. (2000) found that nursery education was seen as important to parents in preparing their children for school. Their role as parents was to hand over their children to those with more expertise. The researchers comment on the positioning of parents and teachers in the discourse about early education: "Teachers and schools are privileged because of their status as guardians of the educational process. They 'know' how to teach and parents do not. They 'know' how children learn and parents do not" (ibid.).

Monitoring Progress and Behaviour

The English government's recent white paper 'The Importance of Teaching' makes several references to the importance of providing "information to parents about how well their child has done and about the effectiveness of schools" (Department for Education, 2010: 11). For schools, *accountability* is the key word. For parents, the requirement is to monitor and, if necessary, intervene. Information for parents in the form of school reports is not new, nor is the publication of data on attendance, exam results and so on. The need for national benchmarks continues, as the white paper states. However, the message is that parents and schools have greater responsibility to ensure that learners make progress. In order to monitor progress, parents will be able to refer to the national curriculum.

> [It] will act as a new benchmark for all schools. It will be slim, clear and authoritative enough for all parents to see what their child might be expected to know at every stage in their school career. They will be able to use it to hold all schools to account for how effectively their child has grasped the essentials of, for example, English language and literature, core mathematical processes and science. (op. cit.: 42)

It is unclear whether schools could be held to account for poor performance in subjects that are less fundamental markers of success as the prized subjects specified as examples. There is no explanation as to how parents will hold schools to account. One rather extreme way would be to set up a rival 'free school', a solution that is unlikely to improve the poorly performing school and not a possibility for most parents.

The role of a parent in monitoring a child was reinforced by the requirement since 1998 for schools in England and Wales to draw up a home-school agreement. These can be used in Northern

Ireland and Scotland, too, although there is no official government policy (Harris, 2009). Home-school agreements usually lay out the school's ethos and remind parents of their legal responsibility to ensure their child attends school. Aside from providing this reminder, the document asks parents to sign up to support the school. There is no legal requirement for parents to sign, and some parents might not be approached, depending on home circumstances. Even so, these agreements are not presented as optional in England and Wales. The document is not legally binding, and there should be no sanctions for refusing to sign (School Standards and Framework Act, 1998).

Getting Involved with Education

Parents have been instrumental in setting up schools in Northern Ireland and England. In Northern Ireland, the parent group All Children Together spent five years campaigning for integrated schools (McKeown, 2013), which must include a balance of Protestant and Catholic pupils, in a bid to encourage greater tolerance of religious difference and a more cohesive society. In England, parents can apply to set up a free school, which provides education for learners of all abilities and is funded by the government but managed independently of the local council.

In Scotland, the Parental Involvement Act was passed in 2006, requiring local authorities to have a strategy for how they will involve parents and to establish a parent council drawn from all parents, known as the parent forum. The parent councillors' roles include supporting management of the school and making representations to the head and the education authority about the school (Scottish Executive, 2006b).

In Wales, a number of initiatives, such as the FAST (Families and Schools Together) and Flying Start programmes, have been put in place to address social inequalities that hamper progress in education and to encourage parental involvement and engagement, although the impact on achievement is uncertain (Egan, 2013). Parental involvement is recommended, nonetheless, and is promoted as being cost-effective (taken to mean relatively inexpensive).

Parents are also expected to be involved in their child's education in England. The research shows that parental involvement in children's learning is a key factor in improving children's academic attainment and achievements, as well as their overall behaviour and attendance… The role of parents during a child's earliest years is the single biggest influence on their development. Good quality home learning contributes more to children's intellectual and social development than parental occupation, education or income. (Department for Education, 2012b)

It has been suggested that this has reached a point where the roles of the teacher and parent are blurred (Gillies, 2012). It is unclear whether the majority of parents, or indeed teachers, welcome the expectation to be more involved. The government's call for greater parental involvement is interesting given the evidence that higher levels of parental *intervention*, which is one type of involvement, are associated with those in professional and managerial jobs (Vincent, 2012). This is not necessarily the kind of involvement that is being promoted by the government. The parental role of providing 'good quality home learning' is cited as the key factor. The rhetoric asks for support of the school and its approach to learning rather than an equal partnership between parents and teachers; thus parental intervention would not count as legitimised parental involvement.

The English government's parenting campaign aims to support families in the early years, specifically up to the age of five (Department for Education, 2011a). Parenting classes extend beyond this age, however; there is an "unmet demand for parenting education aimed at the parents of primary school-aged children. Parents, particularly those in lower socio-economic groups, welcome the provision of parenting education through local primary schools" (Holloway & Pimlott-Wilson, 2012: 6). The researchers also conclude that targeting particular parents is stigmatising and that universal provision would therefore be preferable. 'Good parenting' under these circumstances would be more narrowly defined to fit the social expectations of those in governance, thereby reducing parental rights to choose how a child is raised. As the English government says, "While families must have the freedom to manage their own lives, it is critical that the workforce has the skills to offer evidence-based interventions, including parenting programmes, where appropriate" (Department for Education, 2011a: 60).

More welcome parental involvement could include helping children with language, literacy and numeracy; attending parents' evenings; assisting with events and fund-raising activities; and helping with homework. A report (Moon & Ivins, 2004) prepared for the Department for Education and Skills, as it was then known, indicated that women and lower socioeconomic groups reported feeling more involved. In practice, however, the greater involvement of the latter was in helping with dinner duties and school trips. The main barrier to involvement was work commitments. Half the parents frequently helped with children's homework, although many were not confident about helping, particularly with maths. The report reveals that many parents are trying to help their children in a number of ways, both with the work done at school (of which homework is a small part) and by providing wider educational opportunities, such as visiting museums.

A role that relatively few parents take is that of parent governor. The Department for Education (2012c) states that there about 30,000 governors in England, some of whom are parent governors. They are either elected or appointed to the board of governors, whose roles include

- setting targets for pupil achievement,
- managing the school's finances,
- making sure the curriculum is balanced and broadly based,
- appointing staff, and
- reviewing staff performance and pay (ibid.).

Governors are also responsible for handling complaints and implementing local education authority policy. In England and Wales, parent governors may take the role of parent governor representative (PGR), of which there should be two to five on local-authority education committees in England. The PGRs are elected by parent governors and represent parents' views in an "apolitical way" (Department for Education, 2012d) beyond the school, including at local-authority meetings.

Rights

The Right to Choose

The right to full-time free education from the age of five to the school-leaving age applies to learners rather than parents. Since the Education Reform Act of 1988, parents have had the right to request that their child attends a primary school other than their local one and, similarly, to choose a secondary school, although it may not be possible to fulfil these choices if schools are oversubscribed. A relatively new (June 2010) parental right in England is to set up a free school. In his letter to local authorities, Michael Gove stated that free schools "aim to tackle educational inequality and give greater powers to parents and pupils to choose a good school" (Gove, 2010). Exactly how educational inequality will be tackled by the setting up of free schools is a mystery. Early indications suggested that these schools were oversubscribed (Department for Education, 2011b) as parents vied for limited places. This could have been (or could still be) true of some schools, but the Labour Party claims now that 70 per cent are not full (*The Independent*, April 23, 2014).

Parents also have the right to home educate their children, thereby increasing their responsibility for their child's or children's education. In principle, if the local education authority were unhappy about a child's home education, it could enforce attendance at school or take a child into care. However, there is no requirement for the local authority to monitor or inspect home education. In theory, parents have the right to home educate their children as they see fit, although they do not have the right to free exam entry. Parental choice in terms of a curriculum for home education is likely to be constrained by the practicality of needing nationally recognised qualifications, particularly when these are the usual currency for further and higher education or employment.

Another right parents have is to an education for their children in keeping with their religion. This principle was set out in the 1944 Education Act and established as a human right in 1952:

> No person shall be denied the right to education. In the exercise of any functions which it assumes in relation to education and to teaching,

the State shall respect the right of parents to ensure such education and teaching in conformity with their own religious and philosophical convictions. (Protocol to the Convention for the Protection of Human Rights and Fundamental Freedoms, article 2, 1952)

Parents were also given the right to withdraw their child from religious worship or religious education by the Education Reform Act of 1988. No national statistics are available to indicate how many parents exercise this right. By way of example, there have been no recorded withdrawals in East Sussex (East Sussex County Council, freedom of information request, July 2012). The Humanist Society suggests that many parents may not be aware of this right, which applies to all schools including faith, and of course, even if parents are aware, the right might not be exercised owing to a child's (or parent's) fear of being stigmatised (Humanist Society Scotland, undated). Parents also have the right to withdraw their child from sex education in the United Kingdom, although in England that right has been undermined by the inclusion, in maintained schools, of content about reproduction in science lessons.

Parents have the right of access to their child's school record (or common transfer file), although a school might remove some detail, in which case a parent can ask why that has been done. Censored information is likely to relate to the Data Protection Act. The record includes attendance data, copies of reports, any correspondence parents have had with the school, and information from the local authority. Optional information might be included, such as whether the child has been excluded or information about family background. Data are unavailable on how many parents exercise the right to access their child's record or why access might be requested.

An important area in terms of equality of education is the rights that children with special educational needs or disabilities have. Parents have the right to ask for a statutory assessment of their child's needs, although the system is currently under review in England, where a single assessment process has been proposed to simplify the system (Department for Education, 2011c). This green paper also suggests that families should be given a personal budget by 2014 to manage their child's needs and that they should have more choice in which school their child attends in order to "remove the bias towards inclusion" (5).

The Right to Complain

In relation to state schools, parents can complain directly to their child's school, to the local authority, to the inspectorate, and if all else fails, to the secretary of state for education. Local authorities will hear complaints about curriculum matters and collective worship. In private education complaints should in the first instance be directed to the governing body. A survey of schools about the numbers of parents complaining and the types of complaints found that on the whole few parents complained and that most complaints were about discipline issues and not dealing with bullying (McKenna & Day, 2010). There are no central sources of data for complaints to draw on, and therefore the representativeness of the data cannot be assured. The small-scale survey yielded 124 responses, a replacement for the survey of three thousand English schools that was planned for but not commissioned by the Department for Education. The survey asked schools whether they thought parents might be reluctant to complain. The response from some was that it was not possible to tell. The right source for this information is surely parents and not schools. A point to make here is about the lack of power that parents have to tackle perceived difficulties or injustices.

There is evidence that parents who take their children out of school in favour of home education have concerns about the education system (e.g., Rothermel, 2002). For many parents there is little choice but to accept that they, their children or indeed other parents and their children are the root of any problems, particularly given the sense that complaining can be "a nervous and uncomfortable experience" (Sherbert Research, 2009: 3), at least for what the report refers to as 'harder to reach parents'; there is no reason to think that is less true for other parents even if they have the cultural and social capital (Bourdieu,1986) to pursue their concerns.

Responsibilities

Daniel Monk (2009: 143) states that "parental responsibility and education is a vast subject". Parental responsibility became a legal term in the Children's Act (1989), which defines parental responsibility as "all the rights, duties, powers, responsibilities and authority which by law a parent of a child has in relation to the child and his property" (section 3). The parent may or may not be the biological one. Another person might take parental responsibility or, in the case of teachers, act as a responsible parent would. Parents are legally responsible for what their child can and cannot do until they are 18 (16 in Scotland).

Gilmore et al. (2009) point out that if parents are legally responsible for bringing up a child, then they have some freedom in how they do that. They can also be accountable for their choices and for their children's actions. The rights of parents are not for their benefit but rather for the child's, and although the term *rights* was altered to *responsibility*, legally there is no difference; indeed, the definition of parental responsibility includes *rights* and *duties*. Parents are, then, legally responsible to and for their children, and to other authorities. This is true whether or not they agree with the education system in general or the ethos of their child's school.

Parents are legally required to ensure their child attends school regularly. The precise number of absences that are allowed is not specified. The definition of persistent absence is set at 15 per cent. Unauthorised and high levels of absence are likely to trigger a voluntary parenting contract in England and Wales. Further sanctions might be taken. These are school attendance orders, education supervision orders and penalty notices (Directgov). Schools are responsible for monitoring attendance, whereas parents are expected to tell the school why their child is absent. Up to ten days per year can be granted as authorised absence, including for family holidays, at a head teacher's discretion. Twice as many absences are allowed for holidays by primary schools than secondary (Department for Education, 2012e), if the data are valid. A widely reported survey of two thousand parents by LV= Travel Insurance (2012) indicated that parents are apt to lie about the reason for absence in order to capitalise on lower prices; they are also willing to risk being fined for going against the school's wishes, the amount saved by holidaying off-peak far outweighing the fine of £60.

The amount of freedom parents have is limited by the laws and social expectations of the country or culture they live in. Nonetheless, parents are perceived as responsible for their children's behaviour. Carol Vincent (2012) refers to a survey report in which 81 per cent of teachers held parents responsible for their child's poor behaviour, either because of inadequate parenting or because of family break up or single parenting. The law serves to extend parental responsibility to a child's behaviour in school through parenting orders and penalty notices (DCSF, 2007). These extreme measures may follow the failure of a parenting contract, although that is a voluntary agreement, to ensure a child attends school or behaves well when there.

> This extension of parental responsibility represents a 'criminalising' discourse in two ways. Misbehaviour in school is effectively treated as a 'crime' (the exclusions process attests to this) and parents and children are both held to account and found culpable. (Monk, 2007: 157)

Diminished responsibility can apply to education and crime equally. A school or local authority can decide whether a child's behaviour is because of a special educational need, in which case both parent and child are held less responsible for behaviour. Special educational needs are laid down in policy and law. The need for, say, a more interesting, more varied or more relevant curriculum would not be included in spite of the role those elements have in creating discontent, truancy and exclusion from school. Parental responsibility therefore includes support of the education that is available, and ensuring their child's support, unless a recognised difficulty can be established.

Whilst acknowledging that parents have the freedom to raise their child as they wish, I would not like to imply that all parenting is equally helpful in child development or that parents do not have responsibility for how they bring up their child. There is extensive research that indicates the value of authoritative parenting, for instance, if there is consensus that certain values should be promoted, such as democracy and autonomy. Authoritative parenting is characterised by warmth, responsiveness, promoting controlled autonomy and upholding certain standards of behaviour. Steinberg et al. (1992) found a strong correlation between adolescent achievement and authoritative parenting. Their findings also indicated that parental involvement was more likely to lead to success if associated with authoritative parenting. A recent television programme (*Mr. Drew's School for Boys*, Channel 4) highlighted the effect of less helpful parenting styles (such as authoritarian, laissez-faire, and inconsistent) and the value of both authoritative parenting and teaching styles in managing challenging behaviour and poor learning habits. Over the course of a summer, through a combination of authoritative teaching methods and parenting classes, eleven boys began to display more co-operative behaviour and, importantly, a greater sense of self-worth.

Tensions

The move towards even greater choice in education for some parents could be viewed as a turn against an inclusive model of education, although others may see it as an opportunity to remove barriers to learning for their child. Brahm Norwich, in his book on inclusive education for children with learning disabilities or difficulties (2013), refers to five tensions, the first four of which I suggest apply to parents generally. They are participation-protection, choice-equity, generic-specialist, what exists as real-relative, and knowledge as investigation-emancipation.

The first tension (participation-protection) can be related to the extent to which parents listen and respond to the views of their own children in choosing a school, given that parents might wish to protect them from potential difficulties, such as bullying or lower achievement, although dependent on the amount of choice available. Child protection may reduce the rights of parents with learning difficulties. "This tension—between protecting children and upholding the rights of parents—is real and considerable" (Tarleton et al., 2006). The second tension (choice-equity) is whether it is possible to make a choice system fair, which is dealt with in more detail below. The third tension (generic-specialist) is relevant to parents' views on what is offered by a particular school in terms of faith, curriculum, teaching methods or resources and whether a specialist school would be more suitable. Part of this tension lies in viewing institutions as sites of risk, where parents' strongly held views and hopes for their children might be threatened. The fourth tension (real-relative) concerns what parents view as existing and definable, which could include notions of intelligence and learning difficulties such as dyslexia or 'gifted and talented'. They view their child as 'having' a particular characteristic and therefore see it as their responsibility to respond to 'it' and in a timely fashion.

Choice-Equity

Offering choice to parents can be a source of tension as well as inequality. Parents may disagree on which school is best, either with each other or with their children. Morally, parents may be torn between supporting equity and ensuring their children are not disadvantaged. Gallagher and Smith (2000) report Northern Irish teachers' guilt when sending their own children to grammar school whilst teaching in a secondary school. Much has been made in the press about the hypocrisy of politicians who send their children to schools that confer an educational advantage.

What would constitute a fairer system is contentious. Norwich supports the idea of choice for parents of children with additional learning needs but calls for it to be "appropriately regulated" (2013: 125). That, too, could be contentious of course. The same applies to all children's parents. I would agree with Henricson that "some clarification might be helpful as to the level of autonomy to which a parent is entitled and the circumstances in which it can be legitimately eroded" (2003: 40).

Home-School Agreements

Suzanne Hood (1999) discusses the tensions inherent in home-school agreements in which parents are cast as partners when in fact the balance of power is with the school. In an equal partnership, parents would be involved in drawing up such an agreement. If that were the case, parents might wish to query some of the requirements they are asked to agree to. (See also Henricson, 2003.)

Inequalities

Choice, Equity and (Lack of) Social Mobility

Not all parents have choice, regardless of the right to choose. Very few parents have a free choice of schools. Some have no choice and others a forced or limited choice, particularly those living in rural or island communities or those who lack financial and social capital. The question of whether parents want choice cannot be separated from the rhetoric that tells them they do because an education market drives up standards and therefore the quality of education. The main reasons for choice of school are good academic standards, similar social background, children's friends' choices, and distance (Hansen et al., 2010; Burgess et al., 2009), although there is more choice in urban areas.

Inequalities of choice, which reduce equity in the education system, are a global phenomenon. Many other countries are grappling with how to make the system fairer. Strategies to do so include controlling choice, offering financial incentives to education providers to be more inclusive and providing more information to parents (OECD, 2012). However, a fundamental issue for success in education and equality is how much money parents have, which schools cannot compensate for adequately if at all. Research shows that by the age of three there is already a nine-month difference in school readiness, a gap which widens to an almost two-year difference by the age of 14 (Hirsch, 2007). Since income is related to achievement, Hirsch refers to the cycle of underachieving parents and their children as a chicken-and-egg situation. Other research also shows that the difference in achievement increases after the age of 11 in relation to parental socio-economic status (Sutton Trust, 2011):

> The widening gap after eleven is found to be mainly related to the positive association between the quality of secondary school that children attend and their parents' socio-economic status, SES, which is stronger than the association between primary school quality and parents' SES. (ibid.: 9)

The effect of schools on differential outcomes is not confined to achievement in exams. There are also differences in expectations, aspirations and social skills, which, particularly at a time of high unemployment, will affect the chance of securing work later on. Parents' choice (or lack of choice) of school does contribute to life chances for their offspring, but this is only one cause of inequality. The Millennium Cohort Study data indicate that, at age five, teachers' assessments on a range of measures strongly associate with certain family profiles (Hansen et al., 2010). Higher achievement related to being a girl, born earlier in the year, heavier at birth, read to every day pre-school, and the child of a mother who values stimulation of young children. Lower achievement was associated with having a black mother, a depressed mother, or parents with lower educational achievement and living in social housing. Pakistani and Bangladeshi mothers' children were judged to have better personal, social, and emotional development as well as cognitive skills compared with those of white mothers.

One might think that non-selective education could help to offset inequalities, but this would only be true if no other choice were available and if schools could make up adequately for differences arising from a child's developmental niche. Ward and Eden (2009: 37) say, "comprehensive schooling increased, rather than diminished, inequality" because middle-class parents are able to play the system to their advantage and are more motivated to do so. Middle-class parents feel burdened with the responsibility of choice. They are anxious to weigh up the alternatives, or they would suffer feelings of guilt for letting their child down (Ball, 2003).

Unequal life chances are not just a problem for the United Kingdom. "In no country did the authors find a reduction in mobility differences by family background over time, highlighting the need for more effective avenues to reduce the connection between parental status and subsequent wellbeing" (Sutton Trust, 2011: 11). Parents can be seen as immediately responsible for their children's success or increasing failure in the education system through social factors that are passed from generation to generation. "Parents with more resources—material, cultural, intellectual—are able to give their children a better preparation for entering school" (Hirsch, 2007:10).

Recent reforms to the education system, particularly in England, that allow greater choice will provide the opportunity for some parents to capitalise more than ever on their socially inherited advantage.

The Relationship between School and Home

Parental involvement is implicated in the relationship between what happens at school and what happens in the home. Many parents will have heard the response 'nothing' to the question of what their child did at school that day. Whether parents dig deeper will no doubt depend on the particular parent and on a range of priorities that day or any other day. Parents might be involved with homework, which offers a link between the school and home and a potential link between parent and child, although it can be a source of tension (Solomon et al., 2003). Whether homework has value is contestable.

> The more we move into [the contested territory of homework and parental involvement] the more pertinent the questions it raises. Studies of homework, for example, arrive at very different conclusions, in relation to its negative impact, its neutral effect and its positive benefit. It all depends on the nature, locus and classroom use of homework and, most crucially, the support, encouragement and help of peers and parents in which 'homework' is deeply embedded in the quality of home life. (MacBeath, 2012: 60)

There is scope for further research on the role of parents, who remain silent partners much of the time. There are reports from young people of the varied and subtle roles that their parents play in their education. These roles are part of *habitus*, which refers to "durable, transposable dispositions" (Bourdieu & Passeron, 1977: 179) to think and act in particular ways. An example is included here from my research with John Webber on effective learners by way of illustration. The 17-year-old students talk about behind-the-scenes interactions that may blend or clash with the expectations or advice of the staff:

> They sort of gently advise me, maybe you should do just one hour, do some geography or something. (Male, academic route)

> My mum pushes me most because she wants the best out of me, she wants me to go on to uni so she pushes me quite a lot and encourages me. (Female, vocational route) (McQueen & Webber, 2013: 723)

It is also difficult to see how parental involvement can ever be a true partnership if teachers are viewed as having greater expertise and if they hold greater knowledge about what is required to gain marks or succeed in exams. Further research on how parents help with homework and coursework (including for exam purposes) is warranted. There are many and subtle ways in which parents are involved in their children's success at school, including avoidance of and management of failure. There has been much in the media about too much help from parents (and from teachers and the Internet) with summative work not assessed by public exams. It is very unlikely that all parents read or adhere to the official guidance's imperatives on what help is permissible, imperatives that are difficult if not impossible to monitor. Here is an example:

> You can encourage your child to do well and provide them with access to resource materials. You must not put pen to paper - you must not write the coursework. You can discuss the project with them but you must not give direct advice on what they should or should not write. ("QCA Coursework: A Guide for Parents": 2–3)

Changing how work is assessed may put an end to some parental strategies but will not preclude the development of others. There is much anecdotal evidence to support the idea that parents are giving advice on their children's work, frequently because they are asked to by their children. It can be an enjoyable, collaborative activity for children and parents, one that can support the development of skills through one-to-one interaction and the deployment of parental knowledge and skills. The problem is that advantages and disadvantages are amplified through education work at home, which may include homework.

Parent Voice

Some parents are heard more than others. One grassroots group is Parents Outloud, which aims to give voice to parents. In Northern Ireland the group has, for example, proposed a more flexible school starting age (Northern Ireland Assembly, 2013) and called for more school inspections (BBC, 2014). Those parents who will be heard little if at all are likely to be the ones identified in the Millennium Cohort Study as experiencing poorer educational outcomes for their children—for example, parents with a lower level of education. Cleaver et al. (2013) point out that mental health problems, learning disabilities, substance misuse and domestic violence are not uncommon and can occur together. If the result is "a sense of apathy, blunted emotions and low self-esteem" (199), as the authors suggest, then parents with such difficulties are unlikely to be able to engage effectively or at all with educational issues that affect their children.

Little information is available on the demographic constitution of parent governors, who can be seen as the official voice of parents, or the democratic process of election (bearing in mind that members can be co-opted). However, the process to become a parent governor leaves room for doubt about both of these points. Firstly, parents can self-nominate or be nominated by another parent. The nomination needs to be seconded. This suggests that more confident and socially connected parents will dominate. The proposal should include a personal statement, and a brief look at some of those available online suggests many nominees have professional backgrounds. Some PGs are teachers with children at another school (a teacher cannot be a parent governor in a school if their child attends the same school). Although parent governors represent the views of parents, thereby providing a conduit for others who may not wish or be able to apply, they are not obliged to vote in accordance with those views. However, it is unclear how influential parent governors are, regardless of how representative they are. Further research is warranted to explore these issues. The effectiveness of parent governor representatives (PGRs) has been the subject of research (RISE, 2004); the report suggests that the role of PGR is an important one although effectiveness can be hampered by, for instance, lack of support and local authorities' indifference to the role.

Concluding Comments

Parents have limited rights in education yet are increasingly held responsible for better or worse outcomes. Government rhetoric promotes the idea of parental choice as a right, although in practice this right is severely limited by cultural and social capital. The government's suggestion that parents support existing or reformed educational policy is not supported by evidence. As Hughes et al. say, "If policy-makers genuinely want to maintain that their policies are supported by parents, they must give parents a central role in the decision-making process" (1994: 219). The only parents who have a central role at the moment are those in governance who happen to be parents.

The role of parents in education is extensive in breadth and in length of time, although involvement is tempered by personal and social characteristics. An important role is that of doing the best for their child within an unequal, consumerist system. Stephen Ball says this about good parenting:

> The child must be stretched; talents and abilities made the most of. This is good parenting. Investment in the child begins early and financial capital enables the buying in of services and experiences which play their part in making up the child as an educational subject, constructing them as able or talented, reasonable and reasoning. (2003: 169)

Parents continue to be legally and morally responsible for ensuring their child's compliance with an education that is rarely of their choosing, and few opportunities exist for the majority of parents to debate or challenge the system in productive ways. The English government's plan to "support teachers and parents to set up new free schools to meet parental demand, especially in areas of deprivation" (Department for Education, 2010: 12) is likely to result in the right for some parents to evade structural inequalities for their children rather than to increase equity.

Chapter Summary

This chapter began by pointing out that *parent* is a catch-all term for a person who has a caring role for a child. The many roles that parents take in their child's education from the earliest years through to higher education are described. Although roles are dependent on what is meant by *parent*, normative assumptions about what parents do are outlined under the following headings: "Choosing a Place for Education", "Preparing Children for the Education System", "Monitoring Progress and Behavior", "Getting Involved with Education", and "Supporting or Challenging the System". Government policy hopes to capitalise on parental involvement, and the form that may take is discussed. For some parents, the role of chooser has become more significant, particularly in England. Parents have relatively few rights but are increasingly held to be responsible for educational outcomes. It is acknowledged that parents are highly influential in determining how their children adjust to school and to institutional learning, but home and school can work in opposition rather than collaboratively. One tension discussed is between choice and equity, particularly in England with the introduction of academies and free schools. Other tensions, drawing on Norwich (2013), are participation-protection, generic-specialist, and real-relative. Discussion of inequalities includes which parents' voices are heard; such inequalities are exacerbated by the differential social capital of parents.

CHAPTER 5

Teachers

Teaching in Turbulent Times

Bryan Cunningham (Senior Lecturer in Education, Institute of Education, London)

On being interviewed following the publication of his 2005 memoir *Teacher Man*, Frank McCourt (author of *Angela's Ashes* and *Tis*) said of his years as a teacher in US public schools that he simply hoped he had 'done something useful'. It is surely a sentiment that all of us, no matter which of the sectors of education reviewed in this chapter we are employed in, ought to aspire to being able to realise. One of the apparent obstacles to doing so, however, may arise as a result of the many 'extensive and potentially conflicting roles' that this chapter provides some insight into.

As a professional group, teachers now contend with a huge range of demands on their time, some of which are far from originating in purely curricular or pedagogic concerns. Their responses to such demands are constrained by such factors as internal organisational structures and imperatives, and increasingly by such external forces as marketisation—'choice'—and an increasingly intrusive apparatus and technology of inspection and auditing. From early years to higher education, many would argue that the scope for pursuing, with a high degree of professional autonomy, a *vocation* to teach has been significantly reduced. One may hear the view expressed: 'I seem to spend more time reporting on my teaching than I do actually working in my classroom'. How we actually arrived at such a state of affairs—if we accept its existence—is a long and complex tale that has now been told by far too many authors to acknowledge here.

One writer who seems to me to have offered us especially valuable insights into some of the present conditions under which teachers labour is Eric Hoyle. Perhaps still best known for his highly influential formulation of the notion that there exists in teaching a distinction between *restricted* and *extended* professionality (1974), Hoyle has much more recently pointed to "an endemic dilemma" (2008: 292) in those organisations in which professions such as teaching operate. The nature of this dilemma stems, he writes, "from the interpenetration of professional and bureaucratic (managerial) ways of organising work" (293). This syndrome is arguably one of the all-pervasive features of life in each of the diverse sectors of education making their appearance in this chapter of the present book.

So, how best might teachers—educators at all levels and working in all curricular specialisms—confront such a challenge and meet (or at least appear to comply with) its essential requirements while remaining true to their values and to their vocation? As Hoyle observes, "many teachers are striving to sustain a client-centred professionalism despite a shift towards a system-centred managerialism" (2008: 295). That they are often still able to do so might well be because they have evolved ways of simply working around the many and varied initiatives and diktats (Hoyle & Wallace, 2005) of the current policy frenzy (Hoyle, 1974) and are continuing to put first their learners of whatever age.

For Ron Barnett (2008), some of the ingredients of a successful response on professionals' part to the problems we are faced with in an age of what he has termed 'supercomplexity'

> include a high degree of *vigilance* and the development of a facility to interpret and engage with the *multiple discourses* emanating from all quarters. These discourses can include those of audit, accountability and transparency, those of learner entitlement and well-being, and those arising from within our own communities of professional practice. The last of these is, of course, particularly important for those of us who cling to the hope that we may, despite all other pressures, retain *helping learners to succeed* as our central objective and our prime source of fulfilment.
>
> For the satisfactions of a professional life in education are doubtless still there; certainly the number of 'brightest and best' young graduates competing for places on such a highly selective programme as Teach First would appear to point to the continued appeal of teaching in schools. Meanwhile, in the universities, we can now quite routinely see applications running into the hundreds for an advertised 'early-career' (and therefore not all that highly paid) lectureship in the arts or social sciences. And a character in a John Updike short story, 'Home' (1959), mirrors a perspective that could be held by many other far more time-served educators: 'Though for thirty years a public-school teacher, he still believed in education.'

Teachers and Supporters of Learning

Teachers, teaching assistants, teaching and learning managers, lecturers, professors, readers, instructors, trainers, tutors and mentors all have a role as educators. The term used often depends both on the type of institution or place of learning and the job description for that particular role. Some have a more direct role in the learning process through practice, whereas others may be more involved in the theoretical side. *Teacher* is a general term for an educator but tends to be associated with preschool and primary and secondary schools. The number of teachers has increased greatly in the last fifty years. For example, in 1969, there were 350,000 state primary and secondary school teachers in Britain (Hoyle, 1969). According to various government sources of statistics, there are now approximately 535,000 in the United Kingdom. In England, there are more than 232,000 teaching assistants. Apart from teachers, there are others, too, who play an important part in education, such as library staff and technicians.

Teaching is sometimes associated with pedagogy; *pedagogue* refers to a rather strict, formal instructor. It is interesting to observe, as a teacher educator, that one of the assumptions of many trainee teachers at the beginning of their course is that they should be the fount of all knowledge in their subject and that their role is to somehow transfer that knowledge to their learners, akin to the role of a pedagogue, although usually without the strictness. The term *pedagogue* derives from the Greek *paidagogos*, which refers to what one might call today a (strict) child-minder. Nowadays, most families take direct responsibility for the child attending school with the right equipment. There remain, however, modern parallels with the ancient Greek education system, founded in an unequal society, which will be returned to in the final chapter.

This chapter will provide an outline of the different roles of educators and will tease out similarities and differences between them. Sometimes the terms can be synonymous, while at others there will be clearer divisions. There is, then, the question of what an educator's role should be. In the opening chapter, the confusion over who is responsible for learners' outcomes, given certain political and cultural assumptions, was referred to, and it will be expanded upon in this chapter. The question of what rights educators have, particularly for those with more direct contact with learners, will be addressed.

A number of tensions and inequalities will be highlighted later in this chapter. For example, there are tensions with regard to the requirement or otherwise for a qualification to teach and with regard to the rights of students in relation to the roles, rights and responsibilities of teachers. Berry (2007: 11) refers to "a pervasive and enduring tension" in initial teacher education (teacher training), which is about the balance between practical and theoretical teaching. This is also true of education more widely; it is a tension that underpins the academic-vocational divide. There are inequalities in terms of pay and conditions and the amount of responsibility that each role is either required or assumed to have. These inequalities lead to differences in the perceived status of educators and in the perceived importance of their role to the future success of those in receipt of education. It seems to be the case that higher status is afforded to those who are further from the learner, either physically or in perceived intellect.

Roles

Teachers

It may appear to be obvious to many people what teachers do: they teach. Even if that were their only role, *teaching* has various meanings. It may imply a more content-driven, transmission approach or a more facilitative one. It might be assumed that modern teaching is more student-centred and innovative than in times gone by, a notion that is probably encouraged by images of Victorian schools and portrayals of teachers in literature and the media. For dramatic effect no doubt, fictional teaching tends to focus on the extremes (Ryan & Cooper, 2007). This is also true of fly-on-the-wall documentaries, such as *Educating Essex* and *Educating Yorkshire*, which have recently highlighted the management of demotivated or disaffected young learners. These portrayals do, however, indicate that teachers can have very complex roles that go far beyond passing on knowledge or assisting in its construction.

A teaching qualification, which indicates that a teacher has demonstrated the required level of competence in both classroom practice and written assignments on the theory and practice of teaching, is required in the maintained school sector, except in free schools and academies in England. No teaching qualification is required in the further education (a recent change) or higher education sectors, although it is possible to gain one (see the section on lecturers below).

A brief historical peek at teachers' roles indicates growing complexity over time. Emerson (1842) offers the notion of a teacher as one who teaches functional skills, in today's terminology, and a facilitator—"bound to furnish his pupils with the means of acquiring knowledge" (341). By teaching the three Rs (reading, writing and 'rithmetic), learners are equipped to find out more for themselves. Teachers are, he says, "the keys of knowledge" (ibid.) rather than containers of knowledge. Beyond this, teachers should provide a role model for self-regulatory and morally acceptable behaviour. Similarly, Hawtry (1870) views the role as parental: "the wisest and best" (15) father figure. He also says that "our primary duty [as teachers] is not to impart knowledge but to teach our pupils how to learn". Of course most texts from this period are describing elitist, private education, including boarding school. In 1952, Wolfenden referred to a teacher's role as encompassing a very wide variety or duties and responsibilities. The three main duties are to oneself as a teacher, to the profession (as an upstanding member of the community) and to the child. Hoyle (1969) describes the shift from an emphasis on moral education or upholding moral values to an economic one, following the nineteenth-century industrial revolution and the twentieth-century increase in bureaucratic jobs within large organisations. Teaching specific skills became more important along with the need to select information from a vast and ever-growing pool, leading to more emphasis on teaching than learning. Interestingly, Hoyle predicted a more pastoral role, blurring the boundaries between teaching and counselling or social work.

The idea of a teacher as parent is reflected in the phrase *in loco parentis* (in place of a parent, or more specifically a father), although the official phrase is *duty of care*. This is a legal duty "measured by the standards of a reasonably prudent parent" (Wootton, 2000: 17). A teacher's duties are listed in governmental pay and conditions documents (Department for Education, 2012f, for England and Wales; SNCT, 2001, for Scotland; Department of Education, 1987, for Northern Ireland). Added to these are associated duties (for example, preparing for inspection or attending open evenings).

Self-report of roles is scant compared to the literature on what teachers are expected to do. Duties are likely to include planning and preparing lessons; teaching; managing behaviour; setting and marking work; assessing and recording academic, social and personal progress; preparing for and managing external tests or exams; supervising and protecting students in and out of the classroom; exchanging information with parents (although this is more often in the direction of teacher to parent); preparing for inspections; liaising with external agencies; promoting progress and well-being; monitoring attendance and punctuality; providing one-to-one support or tutorials; covering other teachers' lessons; attending meetings; devising schemes of work; taking part in staff development and reviews; keeping up to date with a subject and with technology; dealing with administration of exam or test requirements; attending open evenings and 'selling' the school or courses to parents and learners; and attending parents' consultation events. There may well be other duties such as resource or staff management, mentoring other staff, and so on. If scaffolding learners, teachers may be supporters, prompters, critical listeners, givers of feedback, simplifiers, motivators, highlighters, and models for learning (Pritchard & Woollard, 2010). Teachers may have to teach a subject that they have relatively limited knowledge of—for instance, biology when they have a degree in chemistry. If teachers are not flexible about what they teach, they could become "a rather expensive luxury", according to Wootton (2000: 5).

In Northern Ireland, teachers may 'cross the threshold' for extra pay if they are "good teachers" (DENI, 2008: 14), with an upper pay scale available if teachers have made a substantial contribution to a school. This is one form of performance-related pay. Some teachers in England and Wales may have Teaching and Learning Responsibility, which attracts an additional payment for schoolteachers. The role must be one that goes beyond classroom teaching. It should focus on teaching and learning and be one that has leadership and enhancement of outcomes within its remit (Department for Education, 2012f). From September 2013, England and Wales are offering, in addition, performance-related pay for being a 'good teacher' or for other reasons such as making a contribution outside the classroom or providing professional development.

Teaching Assistants (TAs)

Teaching assistants can be found in schools across the United Kingdom, although in Scotland they are often called classroom assistants. The latter term could imply a different role, that of a person who is helping the teacher during a lesson in some way as opposed to being involved in teaching. In practice, assistants are inevitably involved in the teaching and learning process through learning support or in some cases whole-class management—hence their inclusion in this chapter. Hammersley-Fletcher et al. (2006) point out that a job description is not always forthcoming, since the role is not clear-cut.

There has been a "huge and unprecedented increase in teaching assistants" (Webster & Blatchford, 2012: 77), particularly in England and Wales since 2003, when a national agreement, entitled Raising Standards and Tackling Workload, stated that TAs could support teachers by providing assistance in the classroom with the teacher present or occasionally providing temporary and short-term cover. The *Times Educational Supplement* online (*TES*, 2013) career information indicates how varied the role can be: assistants may be permanent, temporary, casual, or term time only; they may work with individual learners or small groups; and they may or may not be left to manage a whole class.

The teaching assistant's role, although helpful if not essential to the smooth running of the school day, is worth approximately half the basic pay of a qualified teacher. In England and Wales there are Higher Level Teaching Assistants (HLTA), too, who may have specialist skills and who will take on greater responsibility and thus are likely to be paid more. Scotland introduced classroom assistants in 1998 and allows for one or two levels in its guidance documentation, although one report identified four levels (Equal Opportunities Commission, 2007). Northern Ireland's agreement is similar to England's and Wales's with regard to teaching assistants but does not accept HLTAs "because there is no general shortage of teachers and because their use is seen as reducing the standard of teaching provision" (*Teachers' Pay and Conditions of Service Inquiry*, 2004: 37).

Very often, assistants are likely to be attending to those with special or additional learning needs, including those with English as a second language, and to lower achievers. Some of these learners may have disruptive behaviour or needs that the teacher cannot meet without help. The teacher is thus more able to manage the class. In the introduction to her book, Janet Kay refers to teaching assistants as "the 'glue' which holds together the diverse activities of a busy primary school", the sector in which the majority of teaching assistants can be found (2002: vii).

Lecturers, Tutors, and Trainers (Lifelong Learning and Further Education)

This section describes the roles of lecturers and tutors (sometimes teachers or trainers) who teach in institutions other than schools or universities. University lecturers are dealt with under a separate heading. Some schools have sixth forms (years 12 and 13 of study, when students are age 15–19 approximately). However, more often study at the end of compulsory schooling (approximately age 16) takes place in further education colleges or sixth form centres. Alternatively, young people may be able to find employment or undertake training through apprenticeships. Further education is therefore one form of post-compulsory education, although these terms are often used synonymously. It is now a requirement in England for young people to continue to study or train until the age of 17, and in 2014 that will be until 18.

Perhaps it is obvious that people have always learned and continue to learn throughout life, although use of the term *lifelong learning* is a relatively recent addition to educational parlance. The extent of lifelong learning makes it impossible to provide a simple definition—a 'vain quest' according to Aspin and Chapman (2007: 20). Educators in lifelong learning are often associated with adult education programmes—for example, language, art or computing courses. However, it might be professional development or training for those already employed. In practice, *further education, postcompulsory education* and *lifelong learning* may be used synonymously.

The role of educators in this complex sector varies according to the context. Planning and 'delivering' a course or part of a course or one-off session may apply to all, although it is less applicable to an apprenticeship model perhaps. Little has been written about the role of a teacher in work-based learning. The facilitation of non-formal and informal learning as well as the role of human resource departments in work-based learning are beyond the scope of this book (see, e.g., Bierema & Eraut, 2004; McQueen & Varvarigou, 2010; Hallam et al., 2011). For England, the recent McLoughlin report (CAVTL, 2013) emphasises the importance of expertise in vocational education and training (VET) above a teaching qualification, similar to the situation in universities. The report uses "the term 'vocational teachers and trainers' to include a range of 'teaching' roles including teachers, trainers, lecturers, tutors, assessors, mentors, coaches, and workplace supervisors" (ibid.:13); quality provision is characterised by dual professionals, experts in their field and in teaching. From September 2013, the requirement introduced in 2007 to gain a teaching qualification in England if teaching in further education was revoked (LSIS, 2013), which has implications for professionalism, pay and conditions, and for those providing teacher education.

Educators in further and adult education may have a similar role to the one outlined in the first section on teachers, with less emphasis on supervision and probably more on dealing with low motivation (see, e.g., Wallace, 2007), out-of-class problems such as drug abuse, pregnancy, relationships and, particularly for older learners, illness and bereavement. They are also likely to engage in more discussions about student progression (higher education or employment). Given the age group involved, some educators may view themselves more as a friend than a teacher, or at least as an equal, although it is important to maintain boundaries (see, e.g., Gravells, 2012).

Frequently, the role is less behaviourist and more humanistic. That is, there is likely to be less emphasis on training learners through rewards and punishments, monitoring behaviour and transmitting information, and more emphasis on facilitating learning and supporting learners, an andragogic rather than pedagogic approach. Sessions may be longer (90 minutes or more) than lessons in schools, for which various activities and resources are helpful in keeping the interest of the learners. Thus more time might be devoted to planning and preparing. Malcolm Knowles's text (1980) compares andragogy with pedagogy (see pages 43–44), which highlights some important differences. These include the former's encouragement of autonomous learning and the likelihood of more motivated students with a wealth of useful experience. However, the context is influential, and individual teachers vary in their approaches. Some FE lecturers may view their role as requiring a more traditional, lecture-style approach, which might be because it was how they were taught, because they believe it is the best way to cover a subject in the time given, because they are preparing students for higher education practice, or indeed all of these.

Lecturers, Professors, Tutors, and Readers (HE)

> [The] roles of those who teach in higher education are complex and multifaceted . . . academics have contractual obligations to pursue excellence in several directions, most notably in teaching, research and scholarship, supervision, academic administration and management and, for many, maintenance of standing and provision of service in a profession (such as teaching or nursing). (Fry et al., 2009: 3)

Higher education is often used synonymously with *university*, but higher education courses may be available in further education institutions (see, e.g., Parry et al., 2012). Universities may be referred to as *higher education institutions* (HEI). Professors and readers only work in HEIs, whereas lecturers are to be found in both types of institution. It is not a requirement for a teacher in higher education to have a teaching qualification. No data are currently available to indicate how many choose to train or enter the profession with a teaching qualification, but it can be assumed to be a minority. It is possible to gain a postgraduate or professional certificate (the names vary according to institution) in teaching and learning in higher education. Courses encourage reflection on teaching practice in relation to pedagogic theory. There is no training available for the role of professor, reader or teacher trainer. Universities in the United Kingdom promote staff to these roles. Professors and readers will probably teach less and spend more time than lecturers on researching, publishing nationally and internationally, networking and attending conferences. Professors will most likely have scored highly in the Research Excellence Framework (REF, which assesses the quality of research in HEIs) and may have attracted large amounts of research funding. Promotion to professor relies more on experience in teaching, research and administration than promotion to reader, who will have made important contributions to a subject through publications or other academic work.

The general word for someone who teaches in higher education is *lecturer*. Job descriptions for the role of senior lecturer highlight the importance of having gained external funding for research rather than having greater teaching expertise. It is likely that a senior lecturer would have more management experience and would have published articles or books. The word *tutor* is associated with tutorials. The system at Oxford and Cambridge Universities involves tutorials, which aim to provide a forum for discussion to, amongst other things, "develop students' ability to think and act like a professional in their discipline, like a classicist, mathematician, historian, scientist, or social scientist, rather than like a student 'covering' a syllabus in classics, maths, history or a science" (Oxford Learning Institute, 2012). In other institutions, *tutor* is likely to refer to a personal tutor, which means a lecturer to whom (usually designated) individual students can call upon for academic or pastoral support. In initial teacher education, where trainees are studying in an institution but are on placement in a school or college, tutors monitor trainees' progress, liaise with mentors in the placement, assess trainees' written work and carry out formative and summative observations.

Badley and Habeshaw (1991) suggest that the traditional role of a teacher in higher education, or more particularly a university, was that of an expert or authority on a subject who transfers the information to students, most often by lectures. In addition, teachers have traditionally held seminars or tutorials and acted as facilitators of discussion, sharpening the critical faculties of students' minds. These roles have changed, and Badley and Habeshaw comment on the resistance to some form of teacher training by many lecturers, leading to a lack of preparation for certain roles. These roles include course designer, teacher, resource locator and user, project supervisor, pastoral tutor, assessor, evaluator, administrator and even subject expert. As in other areas of education, roles have expanded with the expansion of educational provision and widening participation. With the shift to a marketised, global education system that is viewed as serving the economy, those working in higher education may be expected to work as those in business do: liaising with business, generating income and networking.

Teaching and Learning Managers

Teaching and learning managers are to be found throughout the sector and across the United Kingdom. Very little has been written about the role, and therefore information has been drawn from personal experience and from job adverts for the role in different types of institutions. Although teaching and learning managers might have been included in the governance chapter, their place here is justified by the more direct role they have in influencing classroom practice. They are also likely to teach. Of course one could say that all teachers and teaching assistants manage learning, but someone with that title is usually part of the senior management team and tends to be involved in developing other teachers' practice (CPD) through training or mentoring. The focus is likely to be on improving results, preparing for inspections and monitoring or enhancing students' experience of the institution. They are also likely to contribute to institutional policies about teaching and learning. Some institutions may encourage innovative approaches to learning, although that depends on the willingness of senior managers to take what might be considered a risk. There may be an emphasis on the use of virtual learning environments (VLEs) and technology in general, for efficiency or educational purposes or both.

Teaching Support (Personal Tutors, Mentors, Student Services, and Counsellors)

The need for staff to support learners' well-being has resulted in the extension of roles in educational institutions as well as the creation of new posts. Frank Furedi (2004) talks of the 'therapeutic turn' that occurred in the latter part of the twentieth century, correctly predicted by Hoyle (1969). Hayes and Ecclestone (2012) expand on the theme, giving examples of how staff in all sectors of the system are required to pay attention to the emotional well-being of their students. For example, in further education, they comment on the "huge rise in counsellors, retention support officers, anger management mentors, personal tutors and learning support managers" (ibid.: 80). The boundaries between these roles can be very blurred. All roles will involve listening, and some will have a more advisory element, too. Since learners may well select someone who they think will be sympathetic to them and who may or may not be the expected or designated staff member, teaching and other staff working in an institution (for example, library staff, technicians, career advisers, caretakers, security and reception staff) could find themselves taking a pastoral role in some situations.

Support for trainee teachers is provided by a designated mentor, although much informal support is likely to be provided by other members of staff in the institution. Whether teachers are training in-house or are on placement whilst studying in a different institution for a teaching qualification, mentors provide support with practice (e.g., planning lessons, devising schemes of work, developing teaching strategies, finding resources, and negotiating institutional systems), carry out observations of trainees and write reports.

Rights

All employees in education have a right to a contract and a job description. Teaching contracts are subject to UK law regarding pay and conditions and to equal rights (Equality Act, 2010). Conditions of service in England and Wales (*Burgundy Book*, 2000) state that teachers have a right to sick pay, maternity benefit and redundancy compensation. Unless otherwise specified in their contract, teachers have the right not to work on Saturdays, Sundays and public holidays, and they must have a reasonably long break within the working day (Department for Education, 2012f). They also have the right not to undertake administrative or non-teaching tasks on a regular basis (hence the increase in teaching or classroom assistants) and not to supervise students during breaks. The same rights are afforded to teachers in Scotland and Northern Ireland (SNCT, 2007; Department of Education, 1987).

Further and higher education lecturers' rights are laid out in employment law and are therefore very similar to teachers'. However, the number of hours of contact time varies, and they are also not restricted to the school day (ATL website). Further education lecturers should have a rest period of 11 consecutive hours and a break of at least 20 minutes within a 6-hour period. Beyond basic employment rights, pay and conditions for research contracts are decided by HEIs (UCU website). Intellectual property rights are afforded to institutions and to individuals, giving them legal ownership of ideas, inventions and writings.

Rights in terms of behaviour management relate in part to the right for a safe working environment. They may be legal rights (e.g., searching for a weapon or drugs) or rights in the sense of expectation (e.g., the right to learn) (Steer, 2009). Article 26 of the 1950 Universal Declaration of Human Rights (United Nations) states everyone should have a right to education, which is not the same as the right to learn within a classroom. Sanctions against individuals who prevent others from learning include exclusion, which a head teacher has the right to enforce. Teachers have the right to punish pupils providing they have the authority to do so, they are in charge of the pupil, and they do not breach legislation on equalities and human rights. Reasonable punishment does not include corporal (e.g., smacking), which is illegal in the United Kingdom. Teachers have the right to discipline pupils for behaviour off school premises and to detain pupils on school premises. Reasonable force can be used to prevent injury or damage, to keep discipline, and to search for items that could cause harm or the possession of which would count as an offence (e.g., knives and drugs) (see, e.g., Department for Education, 2012g).

Responsibilities

Legal responsibilities arise from the universal principle in UK tort law of duty of care, which applies to all professionals, including those working in education. Institutions have a duty of care for their staff and students, and staff have a duty of care for their students. The law states that any professional "is under a duty to exercise reasonable care and skill" (Powell, 1996: 47). In a school context this duty "is measured by the standards of a reasonably prudent parent" (Wootton, 2000: 17) but on school premises. The phrase would apply to non-teaching staff if they were, as it were, *in loco magistri* (in place of the teacher, to mirror the phrase sometimes used for teachers, *in loco parentis*, meaning in place of the parent). All schools must designate a senior member of staff who takes lead responsibility for child protection (NSPCC, 2013), although all staff are responsible under duty of care for child protection. Other laws are also applicable to education staff, including the Equality Act (2010)—particularly part 6, 'Education'—and health, safety, and welfare regulations. *The Bristol Guide* (Lewis, 2007) gives more detail on laws that apply to school teachers.

Beyond statutory obligations, the term *responsibility* crops up frequently with reference to additional duties (extensions to a person's role) and to accountability. Teaching staff may be held accountable for their students' outcomes in virtue of their direct role in managing learning. The degree of responsibility that teachers have or accept is a matter of contention and will be discussed in the section on tensions below.

Continuing professional development as well as taking part in more general staff development is expected in all professions, including teaching. England no longer requires staff in further education to receive mandatory continuing professional development (CPD) training (BIS, 2012); therefore staff once again have greater individual responsibility for this. In Scotland colleges are responsible for providing a minimum of six days of CPD (Scottish government, 2007). In Northern Ireland, CPD requirements are being reviewed, but one proposal is to make CPD mandatory for further education (Committee for Employment, 2013). Continuing professional development beyond a probationary period is the responsibility of teachers in Wales (Learning Wales, 2012).

Tensions

Qualified and Unqualified Teachers

This first point constitutes a systemic tension with implications for inequality. It relates to the requirement or not to hold a teaching qualification. The debate has been fuelled in England by deregulation in further education, academies and free schools. In private schools and universities, a teaching qualification has never been a requirement. It only became mandatory for teachers in further education to gain a qualification in 2007, and this mandate has since been revoked. The idea of teaching as a craft to be learnt in situ rather than studied in separate training institutions has come to the fore. Michael Gove, former secretary of state for education in England, declared that "teaching is a craft and it is best learnt as an apprentice observing a master craftsman or woman" (Gove, 2010). On the other hand, teaching is described in many texts as a profession that upholds professional standards and requires a theoretical grounding that is separate from practice. Recent headlines capture the debate and the opposing views:

- 'Do Natural Teachers Need Qualifications?' (*The Telegraph*, October 25, 2013)
- 'Do Teachers Need to Be Qualified? Don't Ask Such Silly Questions.' (*The Guardian*, October 28, 2013)
- 'Of Course You Don't Need Qualified Teachers in Free Schools.' (*The Independent*, October 31, 2013)

Possible alternatives include providing some form of training for all teachers, including those in higher education; requiring training of no teachers; training teachers in the maintained sector; and conducting all training in-house or in a separate institution or both. One implication of deregulation in the requirement for a teaching qualification is unequal pay. As a rule, for maintained schools in the United Kingdom, the pay scale for unqualified teachers is below that of qualified, but, in England, pay in academies and free schools can be decided by the governing body. Similarly, pay scales are merely recommended for further education (except in Scotland) but are set by colleges.

The former independent professional body for the further education (FE) and skills sector, the Institute for Learning, compiled a set of 'thought pieces' responding to the question, "Should teaching qualifications be left to chance?" (Chowen, 2013). Arguments put forward include the value of dual professionalism (expertise in both a subject and teaching) and the importance of training for FE compared with, say, higher education because of the "stark contrasts in the kinds of roles, responsibilities, accountabilities and indeed in public status between the schools, universities and further education sectors" (46). A further issue is the use of unqualified staff on placement in FE as free labour, particularly contentious given the fees that trainees have to pay (*The Guardian*, 2012). A similar tension exists regarding the use of teaching assistants and cover supervisors as cheap labour. In a survey conducted by the teaching union, ATL, almost a third of the sample of 1,435 support staff in maintained schools in England, Wales and Northern Ireland covered lessons for teachers, doing the same or similar job for much less pay (ATL, 2013).

Practical and Theoretical Tensions

Education texts are no strangers to philosophical terminology from the ancient Greeks, which include *phronesis, episteme, techné, praxis,* and so forth. Teacher education tends to use a paradigm that introduces theory, which is then used in the classroom or as a basis for critical reflection. One of the arguments for deregulation is that the most useful knowledge is *phronesis,* or practical wisdom. One difficulty that can arise is that what might be considered productive practice in theory clashes with the reality of a particular class in a specific institution. For example, trainee teachers in further education may be encouraged to question the presentation of information on PowerPoint slides, mindlessly copied by students, only to find that other teachers and their mentor use the approach because, they are told, there is so much 'to cover'. Thus *episteme*, which can be defined as "context-independent knowledge" (Kinsella & Pitman, 2012: 2) or theory, is "washed out" (Korthagen, 2001: 3) by *techné* or "context-dependent . . . craft knowledge" (Kinsella & Pitman, ibid.).

This tension pervades the education system: between individual teachers, who may be more or less disposed or have more or less freedom to avoid the transmission model of teaching; between teacher and managers when grappling with raising standards and quality assurance; for trainee teachers who are confronted with challenges to their attempts to apply episteme or to resist the institutional techné; for teachers who wish to improve their practice but are concerned about accountability for outcomes; and for teacher educators who must decide how to balance the different types of knowledge.

Michael Gove commented that "you learn how to be a great teacher by observing already existing great teachers" (Education Committee, 2010). However, a 'great teacher' is likely to be narrowly defined by easily measured outcomes, and that great teacher may not be as great with all students in all contexts. In-house training will lead to cultural reproduction of practice, which often has short-term goals. For example, some teachers in secondary schools have been accused of teaching to the test and spoon-feeding, either because they choose to or are forced into being more concerned about results in their institution than with what might benefit the student in the future. Coffield (2014: 3) states the result for learners strongly: "[Students] binge on large amounts of information and then, in government-induced bouts of vomiting, otherwise known as national tests, they spew it out." Although some staff are resistant to encouraging this state of affairs, Coffield points out that this tends to take the form of grumbling rather than pursuing constructive action to change it. Teachers can be placed in an awkward position because they are required to uphold standards in a way that may clash with the approach to learning that they value and know, from theory, to be productive. This is where the role of a teaching and learning manager is implicated (see preface to the chapter on learners by John Webber). Rather than emphasising techné and phronesis, as Gove is wont to, Oancea and Orchard (2013: 82) suggest a 'good teacher' represents a combination of "theoretical knowledge (*episteme, theoretike*), technical skill (*techne*) and practical wisdom (*phronesis*)".

Emotional Well-Being and Achievement

The conflation of teaching with therapeutic practice has been referred to earlier in this chapter. For England and Wales in 2003, the Labour government introduced Every Child Matters (ECM), applicable to young people from birth to age 19, a policy that developed from concern about the welfare of a minority but added to a more humanistic approach to education that emphasises personal growth through nurturing and facilitating rather than suppressing and training. ECM included teachers, who should be able to see their role in relation to other professionals, as part of the support network. Teachers might be the first to notice a problem or be seen as negligent if they fail to spot it. Similar policies have been implemented in Scotland and Northern Ireland. For instance, Curriculum for Excellence "emphasises the importance of nurturing learners to help them develop the knowledge and skills they need for positive mental, emotional, social and physical wellbeing at school" (Scottish government, 2013). Since the coalition government came to power in England, the term *Every Child Matters* has been dropped and the five outcomes replaced with 'help children achieve more' (Children & Young People Now, 2010). For teachers, the tension is partly related to balance (how can children be safely exposed to risk and challenge?) and partly to beliefs about the nature of learning (do children need to feel safe in order to learn?). Inevitably there are theories that support different positions.

However, it might be useful to distinguish between two kinds of well-being: hedonic (pleasure) and eudaimonic (flourishing). The hedonic view of happiness is based on avoiding unpleasant experiences and achieving a sense of subjective well-being. Intuitively this might seem like a reasonable basis for learning. The other kind of well-being is not about short-term happiness or comfort but rather living a life that accords with particular values (Ryan & Deci, 2001). There is a tendency to view the former as less productive for achievement, with its emphasis on instant gratification and less controlled emotion, compared with the latter kind of well-being that can derive from deferred gratification and suppressed emotions, traditionally associated with the Protestant work ethic. Perhaps ironically, self-regulation, the rational approach of delayed gratification, and emotional suppression supposedly "work together to create a rich and powerful, imaginative inner life within the individual, the necessary prerequisite for a 'romantic' personality" (Campbell, 2005: 222). Differences in learners' behaviour and aspirations have considerable implications both for how teachers manage their learners and for students' notions of possible selves and imagined futures (see the chapter on learners). Even so, Furedi (2004) questions the therapeutic turn towards suppression of extreme emotions, however well-intentioned, because it encourages tolerance of injustice and oppression. Dealing with negative emotions that view the problems as located within the individual (or family) diverts attention away from the social, including institutional, conditions that created them.

Responsibility, Accountability and Blame

Who is responsible for outcomes for learners? Are teachers at all levels of education responsible for motivating students? It would make educators' lives much simpler if the answer to the first was 'learners' and to the second 'no'. In fact the answers depend on one's beliefs about the purpose or purposes of education, the role of teachers in relation to purpose and whether individual differences in ability and motivation are more or less fixed. Very recently, Boris Johnson, current mayor of London, made the provocative comment that individuals are "very far from equal in raw ability" (BBC News, December 1, 2013), refuelling an age-old debate about natural talent and thus potential. However, the point is not whether there are differences between people but whether individuals can develop an incremental theory of ability. Boris Johnson's statement expresses an entity theory of fixed ability (see, e.g., Dweck, 1999).

Laurillard (2002: 18) makes this comment about university lecturers, although the point is relevant to all education:

> Blame-the-student is a comfortable theory of teaching. If students don't learn, it's not because there is anything wrong with the teaching, it's because they are incapable, unmotivated, foreign or the possessors of some other non-academic defect which is not the teacher's responsibility to correct . . . that is precisely the *challenge* for teachers to teach well, not their excuse for poor teaching.

Biggs and Tang (2011) refer to the transmission, blame-the-student approach as a level 1 theory of teaching. Level 2 teachers also use a transmission model but try to find ways to put across understanding, not just information. The approach shifts the deficit onto the teacher rather than the learner. Level 3 teaching is student-centred and is focused on what learners do: "No longer is it possible to say: 'I taught them, but they didn't learn'" (19).

Miller (2001) offers different types of responsibility. Teachers' resistance to student-centred teaching could be viewed as denying a remedial responsibility for something that they did not cause, or it may be a problem with capacity, that is, lack of time or skills. There is a difference, he says, between immediate and final responsibility. In the context of education, teachers may not have created the difficulties they are faced with or have the power to change them in the future; thus they have immediate but not final responsibility, if the purpose of teaching is to help others learn rather than to tell people what you know.

Inclusion: Removing and Creating Barriers

The tensions here are a result of greater recognition of diversity and integration of learners with special educational needs. The point also relates to what teachers are accountable for, to notions of ability and to the well-being–challenge dichotomy. There are few who would argue against the principle of inclusion, which refers to removing barriers to participation. "It is the acceptance of difference that is the hallmark of inclusive practice" (Tilstone et al., 1998: 23). In practice, it is not easy to achieve, partially the result of inadequate training or professional development, Rouse and Florian (2012) suggest. Removing barriers to allow equity in terms of access does not equate to equality of outcome and can raise awkward questions. For example, is it possible to adjust a course sufficiently, either for practical or ethical reasons, to meet the needs of all? Can someone with severe dyslexia, for instance, provide an adequate learning environment for a subject that demands a high level of literacy, such as English? It is one thing to accept difference and another to find a way to cater for it through 'reasonable' adjustment. As a consequence, barriers to accessing a course of study may be removed, but progression on courses can be compromised.

One of the difficulties identified in both primary and secondary schools by one research project (MacBeath et al., 2006) was that roles and responsibilities for those supporting inclusion are not aligned clearly with particular job titles; furthermore, the latter do not indicate anything about training for the post. Another difficulty is the amount of responsibility allocated or assumed by teaching assistants, which can exceed their expertise. An unintended consequence is that barriers to learning may inadvertently be created.

> In the absence of relevant training TAs tend to play a 'mothering' role (there are very few men), developing a close and caring relationship which can easily become one of dependency. Without expert support they lean more to a nurturing than a learning role and find it difficult to extend challenge and risk taking. There can also be a tendency for TAs to 'isolate' 'their' child from group or whole-class learning contexts. (61)

Teaching and Research in Higher Education

Balancing both aspects of working in higher education can be difficult, not least for universities that are renowned for their research, such as the 24 universities in the Russell Group (2013). Various contributions to a recent live, online chat (*The Guardian Professional*, 2012) indicated that a tension remains in balancing the two. Points included the idea that concentrating on teaching indicated weakness in research and the need to contribute to the Research Excellence Framework (REF, 2012) to be a credible academic and for the benefit of the institution. To progress in higher education, there is the expectation that staff will make successful bids for funding, although this is a very time-consuming process. In short, when there is not enough time to excel in all aspects, it is necessary to prioritise one thing above another. What tends to be prioritised is research because it attracts greater esteem and is viewed as "the true discriminator" in promotion (Drennan, 2001: 177).

Inequalities

Gender

Inequalities tend to cluster, rather than being confined to one identifiable group, although statistical analysis is usually by one characteristic—hence the separation here. The younger the age of the learner, the more education is dominated by females. The most recent published statistics (2011–12) indicate that there are at least twice as many qualified women teachers as men (see table below). However, in early years and primary education, the proportion is almost six females to one male. In further education females are only slightly outnumbered by men, but in higher education over 60 per cent of teaching staff are male.

HESA statistics reported by *Times Higher Education* (*THE*, 2013) reveal that there are over three times as many male professors as female in England and Northern Ireland, over four times as many in Scotland, and over five times as many in Wales. However, differences vary greatly between institutions. There are equal numbers at the Institute of Education, London University, for instance, but more than five times more male professors than female at Cambridge University. There is also discrepancy between full- and part-time teaching staff. For instance, in higher education in 2011, although just under half of full-time staff were female, 67 per cent of part-timers were female (HESA).

The differences in who does what and where in education would not raise equality issues if they were a result of free choice and if status, pay and conditions were equal—but inevitably this is not the case. A survey carried out by the *TES* (2010) indicates male teachers are paid more on average than female. The difference can

Table 5.1 Qualified teachers by gender and school type (rounded figures, in thousands)

	Public sector school type	England	Wales	Scotland	Northern Ireland
Female					
	Nursery & primary	135	9	18	6
	Secondary	104	7	13	6
	Non-maintained mainstream	33	1		0
	All special	9	0	1	1
	All schools	**281**	**17**	**32**	**13**
Male					
	Nursery & primary	25	2	2	1
	Secondary	73	5	9	3
	Non-maintained mainstream	22	0		–
	All special	3	0	0	0
	All schools	**123**	**7**	**11**	**4**

Source: Table adapted from the Department for Education (2013b)

be explained by the positions held, with men having better paid posts, which women either choose or are expected not to apply for. Similarly, in higher education, figures for 2011–12 show a gender pay gap of between 5 per cent (Scotland) and 8 per cent (Northern Ireland) for professors (UCU, 2012).

A report on classroom assistants in Scotland (Equal Opportunities Commission, 2007) reveals that most assistants are women and that the job is undervalued and underpaid relative to assistance jobs undertaken by men in other settings.

> The work done by classroom assistants provides a valuable contribution to children's learning and development. However, this investigation has found that because of the nature of their work, their desire to work with children and the perfect fit for many working

mothers, classroom assistants are a classic illustration of how work associated with women's traditional domestic and/or caring role is undervalued. Classroom assistants, therefore, can often be described as both 'labourers of love' and 'captives of love'. (7)

Race, Colour and Ethnicity

Figures for 2012 indicate that 93 per cent of teachers in England in publicly funded schools are white, 2 per cent are black, 3.3 per cent are Asian and 1 per cent are of mixed ethnicity (Department for Education, 2013c). The percentage of these groups in the population in England and Wales are 86 per cent, 3.3 per cent, 7.5 per cent and 2.2 per cent respectively (Office for National Statistics, 2012). If the discrepancies are a result of free choice of career, then the figures say little about inequality. However, there is inequality in who has the best- and worst-paid jobs. The higher-paid jobs (head teachers and deputies) are held by white British, whereas unqualified teachers are more likely to be Asian, black and mixed race (Department for Education, 2013c). Similar inequalities can be found in higher education statistics (see, e.g., Equality Challenge Unit, 2009). Heidi Mirza talks about the relative invisibility of black, female academic staff, except "when our bodies help higher education institutions achieve their wider moral and ethical goals, and to appeal to a wider global market" (2009: 130).

Concluding Comments

Teachers have extensive and potentially conflicting roles, leading to tensions in their purpose. The roles have become increasingly maternal, or at least there is pressure to be more nurturing than is the case with traditional paternalism, particularly for those in secondary, further and higher education. A combination of the influence of humanism on the support for human development, the demand for better results and for equality, the conflation of learners' rights with an entitlement to succeed, and, in higher education at least, the expectation of a particular kind of service in return for fees paid has put more pressure on all those with a role in supporting learning. This has led to various degrees of compliance and resistance, and to much debate. Similar tensions relating to accountability, responsibility and the best approach to teaching are reported beyond the United Kingdom (see Marble et al., 2000, for instance). Helping students to learn is not equivalent to helping students to succeed, at least not in the short term. The difficulty lies in managing learning over time, as students move from one teacher to another or from one institution to another. Teachers are only held officially accountable for immediate outcomes, even though the effects of 'good' or 'less good' teaching can be very long-lasting. I am not suggesting that accountability should be extended but rather that immediate accountability has limited value. It is all too easy to make teachers "responsible for compensating for the shortcomings of society" (Leaton Gray, 2006: 98).

Chapter Summary

There are many different jobs that involve teaching. These include the jobs of teachers, lecturers, teaching assistants, work-based trainers and mentors. The roles of all those involved in teaching are manifold and have become increasingly complex to the point that the boundary between different roles is often blurred and a source of tension. One example is the distinction between a teacher and a teaching assistant. Another is where the line should be drawn between teacher and unqualified social worker or counsellor. Teachers' rights are contained in policy documents, although the majority of rights relate to employment law. Their responsibilities, like their roles, are considerable and part of accountability in education, which is one of the tensions explored. Inequalities that persist for teachers in education include gender and ethnicity, which are associated with different types of work and opportunities for progression. In spite of the many difficulties that teachers face, I would agree with Bryan Cunningham's suggestion in the preface that teaching can be a source of fulfilment through helping learners to succeed. However, a considerable challenge for those involved in teaching is how to help learners to succeed in the long term and to develop good learning habits rather than foster what Frank Coffield (2014) refers to as 'bulimic learning'. One of the dangers of in-house training for teachers is the development of institutional habitus that can lead to a narrow form of learning and a blinkered view of the role of the teacher in promoting it.

CHAPTER 6

Tensions and Inequalities Revisited: Roles, Rights, Responsibilities and Recognition

The Role of Recognition in Education

Paddy McQueen, Postdoctoral Research Fellow, Queen's University, Belfast

Given its almost intractable complexity, which philosophical concepts and frameworks can help us to navigate our way through the theoretical minefield that is the state of contemporary education theory and practice? One particularly promising candidate, I would suggest, is that of 'recognition'. This concept, which has steadily gained traction within political and social theory over the last decade or two, is drawn from Hegel's philosophy of consciousness and is used to denote the idea that the individual is constituted through his or her interactions with those around him or her. Specifically, it is in being recognised that we come to form a sense of self and to assign value to our identities and lives. This not only highlights the fact that the individual is constituted intersubjectively, thus moving us away from the atomism underpinning much liberal theory, but also suggests that we can only come to view ourselves as autonomous, responsible individuals who are worthy of respect through being recognised as such by appropriate people in appropriate ways (Honneth, 1995; Taylor, 1994).

What, then, does recognition theory offer in terms of understanding and responding to the tensions and inequalities within current educational theory and practice? Firstly, if the aims of education are to promote the autonomy of the learner and to produce responsible, valuable citizens, then we need to reflect on how learners are recognised both interpersonally and institutionally (Stojanov, 2010; Giesinger, 2012). In particular, does the recognition that learners receive contribute to their development as autonomous, independent and self-respecting subjects? This highlights the importance of how teachers relate to learners and how learners relate to one another. Significantly, recognition theory emphasises the importance of mutual recognition. If I am to see myself as, say, an autonomous, responsible subject, then I must be recognised as such. However, this recognition is only of value if I consider the recogniser to be a competent judge. This means that I must recognise the recogniser as someone who is capable of conferring recognition. Only in this way can satisfying relations of recognition take place.

This underlies the important difference between someone acting in an authoritarian rather than an authoritative manner. We are unlikely to value the recognition of an authoritarian teacher, whereas one who acts authoritatively might be someone whose recognition matters to us. One conclusion to draw from this idea is that classrooms must foster an environment in which the learners are able to recognise the authority of the teachers as legitimate, whilst in turn the teacher must recognise the learner as a being worthy of being esteemed and respected as an autonomous, responsible being. This stresses the importance of interpersonal relations within the classroom, especially if the aims and purposes of education are to be satisfactorily achieved. The demands placed on learners and teachers are often incompatible with the ways that they are actually recognised by teachers, governors, politicians and institutions, which can explain some of the tensions that arise within education. Furthermore, forms of disobedience or resistance on the part of both learners and teachers could be explained, at least in part, by the fact that they do not feel that they are receiving the recognition that they deserve (Honneth, 2007).

Recognition is also instantiated through the awarding of grades and prizes, which represent indicators of esteem and success (McBride, 2013). The difficulty with forms of esteem recognition is that esteem is a comparative concept; one can only be esteemed at the expense of others. For example, my obtaining a grade A is only meaningful as a form of recognition if there are others who do not obtain a grade A. This underpins an important inequality within education, insofar as it is not possible to offer equal esteem recognition to everyone. One response to this situation is to offer alternative forms of esteem recognition for educational achievements, such as awarding additional grades based on effort. Whilst this may help counter the tension between success and failure, the problem is that different forms of esteem recognition are not themselves recognised as equal—hence the difference in worth attached to vocational and academic pathways. This is also reflected in the ways that educational institutions are unequally valued. The levels of recognition attached to particular schools, colleges or universities (such as Eton and Cambridge) mean that their grades are worth more than equivalent grades obtained from less prestigious institutions. This underpins the 'market' dimension of the current educational system, in which institutions are ranked according to a competitive market economy of esteem. This ensures a hierarchy amongst learners.

The idea of certain forms of recognition being inescapably comparative suggests that a certain form of inequality and basic tensions within education are inevitable. Thus, rather

> than attempt to eliminate such inequalities and tensions altogether, we can instead reflect on the ways in which esteem recognition might unfairly favour certain social groups or identities. For example, particular bodies of knowledge (such as literary traditions or types of music) might be privileged within the curriculum, with the result that the opportunities for obtaining positive recognition are greater for those individuals connected with these bodies of knowledge. Furthermore, we can strive to reduce the effects of socioeconomic factors that might prevent people from having an equal chance of obtaining recognition for their academic endeavours. This will not solve the inequalities inherent within any system of evaluation, which the education system clearly is, but it might make us feel more accepting of such inequalities. Finally, whilst we cannot all be recognised as equally successful in education, we can all be recognised as autonomous and responsible learners. Thus, moving the focus away from the teleological concern with grades and future success and toward a more holistic focus on the individual's cultivation of self-confidence and self-respect might help reduce the saliency in later life of the differential valuations accorded individuals based largely on their exam transcripts.

The preceding chapters indicate the complexity of the education system in the United Kingdom and highlight some of the tensions and inequalities that exist between what different elements do, the rights that they have in the process of doing or being, and the responsibilities that they are burdened with or embrace. It should also be apparent that each of those involved in education, whether in governance, teaching, parenting or learning, has extensive, diverse and sometimes conflicting roles. The discussion has centred on the system, or rather systems, in place now in the United Kingdom. In this chapter, some of the themes will be explored further, and the question of whether education could be improved, and if so in what way, will be considered.

The following points have been selected for further discussion, with a particular focus on how they relate to the underlying purpose of education:

- Responsibility, autonomy, accountability and choice
- Vocational and academic pathways
- Equality and equity

Responsibility, Autonomy and Choice

I began this book with questions about responsibility and roles, having witnessed and heard of teaching and learning that demanded greater responsibility to be taken by learners and times when teachers took over the role of the learner in an attempt to help learners succeed. What kind of responsibility is involved in these examples? In the opening chapter, a number of synonyms were offered. These were *burden, blame, liability, accountability, constraint, duty,* and *encumbrance*. Most of these have negative implications. Parent.org (2014) refers to 12 forms of responsibility, most of which can be interpreted in a positive way. They are:

- Being accountable
- Exercising self-control
- Planning and setting goals
- Choosing positive attitudes
- Doing one's duty
- Being self-reliant
- Pursuing excellence
- Being proactive
- Being persistent
- Being reflective
- Setting a good example
- Being morally autonomous

If teachers want learners to be more responsible, then they could be referring to one or more of these different interpretations of the word *responsibility*. In the example given in chapter three, Learners, of the higher education student who sought help, the lecturer was perhaps expecting self-reliance whereas the student, I would suggest, was being proactive in seeking help. In other words, the tension was created by two different forms of responsibility. What are teachers responsible for? That depends both on perceptions of a teacher's duty and the teacher's position in an institution. For instance, qualified teachers could be said to have greater responsibility than the majority of teaching assistants because of their wider role. University lecturers may perceive their role as an expert in a subject rather than as someone who directly helps students to learn.

The first point to make is that discourse in policy documents and rhetoric as well as in institutions uses terms such as *autonomy*, *rights*, *responsibility* and *accountability* that are ill-defined. By this I mean that there is an assumption that each term has only one interpretation and that there will be a shared understanding of its meaning. The examples above illustrate this. Another example is that the UK government has signed to guaranteeing the right to an education, but, beyond some basic pointers regarding what that education might consist of, it is very much open to a range of provision. The Convention on the Human Rights of the Child proposes a utopian situation where, amongst other things, children are treated with dignity, develop their potential, develop respect for others, and are prepared for a responsible life in a free society. What would a responsible life in a free society look like? A responsible life is often associated with an autonomous one. Autonomy is valued in the United Kingdom, encouraging the idea that individuals can determine their future and act to realise their goals. Without such autonomy, different options in life are just "mirages of possible experience" (Kupfer, 1990: 2). This is very often the case as apparent choices become narrower and very often socially reproductive, whereby the skills, interests and possible futures of one generation are passed on to the next.

However, autonomy can be defined in different ways. There is a difference between acting independently according to one's own rules (the Greek origin of the word) and regulating oneself in relation to existing rules. The latter type of autonomy is the one demanded by teachers, whereas young people often strive for the former. Furthermore, autonomy can be divided into weak and strong autonomy. Weak autonomy involves choosing from a range of "approved and tolerated ends" in a particular society (Winch, 1999: 78), whereas strong autonomy promotes the opportunity to define one's purpose, regardless of societal norms and expectations. However, the difficulty with strong autonomy is that it promotes "inviolable rights to choose" (ibid.: 79). Although in principle this would appear to be desirable, it is a logically fallible argument. For one thing, each individual's choice affects what other people do, which is likely to weaken their autonomy. England has created both a tension and an inequality in promoting a stronger form of autonomy through the possibility of a free school.

Related to autonomy is liberty, which Berlin divides into negative and positive (1969). Negative freedom refers to what can be done without interference, one aspect of a free society, whereas positive freedom refers to the source of control and self-mastery. It is important that policy which seeks to deregulate education and to increase institutional autonomy distinguishes between the different meanings of autonomy and liberty, assuming there is to be any regulation at all. There has been no suggestion in the United Kingdom that education should be completely deregulated, which would be a form of negative freedom (negative in the sense of absence of control).

It would be helpful to have more overt political and ethical discussion of the meaning of autonomy, liberty, accountability and responsibility in institutions. Indeed, young children are often fascinated by such ideas but are dependent more on their parents than schools for opportunities to discuss them, and in turn on the interest and knowledge of parents. The curriculum for Personal Development and Mutual Understanding (Northern Ireland, 2007) offers the potential for that kind of discussion, although it is unclear how sophisticated an understanding of philosophy and politics is required to 'deliver' the curriculum and whether teachers in any part of the United Kingdom are adequately prepared for such debate. A prescribed curriculum can counter possibilities for exploring meaning by defining what must be covered, which often leads to restricted teaching methods.

The idea of a free society, referred to in the Convention on the Rights of the Child, needs further consideration and definition. Butler (2013) promotes the idea of a free society that permits any action providing it does not harm others. In a free society, one is not "coerced, directed, threatened, intimidated, pressurised, imposed on, interfered with or manipulated by others" (20). However, these terms can be fundamental to a great deal of the education process, not least because it is essential to provide structure and organisation when a large number of people inhabit a confined space. A paradox in education is that constraint in the early years, when rational thinking is assumed to be insufficiently developed, is a requirement for eventual freedom (Marshall, 1996). The assumption here is that young children are incapable of rational thought and of making rational choices (which is not necessarily the case—their rationality just may not match that of adults), and of course that autonomy is dependent on rationality. It is inevitable that education in its broadest meaning will instil dominant values, which includes the extent to which formal education is a public service rather than a private good. In order for society to be free, there needs to be negotiation over or insistence on how that freedom is to be acquired. The ethos of an institution is very important in determining the kind of autonomy that develops in its learners. Some resort to more authoritarian than authoritative approaches to put in place necessary boundaries of behaviour, which often leads to the resistance discussed in the chapter on learners. There can be a tension between the kind of coercion that is used in homes and the kind adopted by schools. Parents as well as learners could be included in open discussion of coercive practices.

The thorny issue of what education might look like in a free society continues to be debated (see, e.g., Machan, 2000). It was weighed up in 1945 by the Harvard Committee in the United States. The report points out that schools (and other educational institutions) "cannot do everything. When they attempt too many tasks, they sometimes fail to do any of them well" (Harvard Committee, 1945: 170). What they should do, it says, is provide a space in which to develop thinking away from everyday life and a basic curriculum (English, maths, and science) that can lead to different paths in life. Readers are also reminded that liberalism in education and education in liberalism (which they propose) are not the same thing. Liberalism in education is about individual choice, whereas education in liberalism exposes people to "truths comprising the goals of the free society" (57). An important question for formal education is what it should do within society. At the moment, it dominates the landscape in terms of personal, social and moral development, at the same time as it attempts to instil knowledge and skills in learners. Added to this is the threat of failure through the requirement to be accountable on particular measures, which can induce a formulaic approach to teaching and learning. It could be time for institutions to concentrate on some kind of core business, as it were, with boundaries regarding the role of the teacher. The role of teacher as subject specialist, first and foremost, has been eroded. Indeed, the extent of many teachers' roles has become untenable, which can lead to burnout, to meeting demands at a suboptimal level, or to prioritising certain aspects above others.

Autonomy has also been referred to in earlier chapters in terms of governance and accountability, with particular focus on how autonomous institutions can be in relation to quality assurance (inspections) and how independent the inspectorate is. Greater institutional autonomy exists for private institutions and English academies, although still within a system of predetermined quality assurance. Waldegrave and Simons (2014) recommend inspections that are founded more on self-assessment than external assessment in England. Indeed, *self-regulation* is often used synonymously with *autonomy*. However, in the same report another recommendation is made, which is that 'outstanding' judgements would only be permissible if schools were to collaborate with other schools for the purposes of improvement. This requirement counters another synonym, *independence*. Gilbert (2012: 23) also calls for school-led accountability that is "professionally owned rather than . . . seen as externally imposed". That would require greater trust in institutional governance and educators and the kind of cooperation and collaboration that is best served by valuing the time it takes to do it well. Most institutions are under considerable pressure to cope with the many demands on their time; rarely do reforms lead to a reduction in workload—most often the opposite.

Perhaps a free society would eventually abandon any attachment to grades and accountability, but some measure would presumably be required to allow prospective customers to choose between the various options in the marketplace. The suggestion that markets are good because they create value and lead to more efficiency and improvements to prevent customers going elsewhere is, according to Orfield and Frankenberg (2013), flawed. This is because a perfect market is a theoretical idea more than a reality, "competition can produce a race to the bottom" (46), and efficiency does not equate with equity. Furthermore, stability and sustainability are in doubt, which is the case now as some schools prosper and others decline. The authors suggest that integration theory is a better option, requiring a regulatory approach to who attends which school. Admissions policy can ensure a mixture of students, but it is not just about managing initial choices. Integration is central to the integrated school's curriculum and ethos. As they point out, life for the better off is not enhanced by inequitable education opportunities because of the negative effect of inequality on society in general.

An alternative would be to remove choice altogether. There are arguments for and against the retention of selective and private (fee-paying) schools. Arguments for private education include valuing a liberal society that permits choice in how money is spent as well as in how one's child is educated (as laid down in the Declaration of Human Rights), offering a strongly academic education that would not be of interest to all, and setting high standards. Arguments against dual provision include the following. It is inequitable and dependent on ability to pay rather than merit, socially divisive, and removes to the private sector young people who could make a positive contribution to state schools. Some of these arguments apply to selective education, too. Some grammar (academically selective) schools are state maintained. In England, there are 164, for instance (Coe et al., 2008), for which there are selection criteria based on a particular kind of merit.

Choice usually refers to parents, and perhaps their offspring, selecting a type or location of school, college or university. There are other choices possible that are the responsibility of governance and educators. For example, the school day might be structured very differently so that there are very few core lessons and the rest of the time is devoted to activities and interests selected by learners, which could be less dependent on traditional modes of delivery and planned outcomes. One of the proposals set out in the Butler Act (1944) was for part-time education from the age of 15, although it was never implemented. What young people would do with the rest of their time is potentially concerning of course. The English government is raising the age of participation to 18 in England by 2015. This will include those who have already found education to be unsatisfactory. A report on the green paper proposing the change suggested that either attendance should be based on wanting to attend, in which case provision would need to be a magnet that offered appropriate choices, or robust enforcement would be needed (Spielhofer et al., 2007). Whether the change would be successful would depend on the quality of provision, including opportunities for apprenticeships and opportunities for paid work when not in education or training.

Mention has been made elsewhere in the book of Summerhill School because it is a rare example of an educational establishment that embraces freedom and reduces the tension between coercion and autonomy. The book *After Summerhill* (Lucas, 2011) recounts the lives of some former participants. Attending lessons is optional, and for many years there was no preparation for exams, although that has now changed. The role of the teacher was that of enthusiastic expert so that "education was caught rather than taught" (109). A similar role is referred to by Harper (2013) with reference to outstanding further education teachers. The cooperative approach at Summerhill led to a community that managed a balance between power and freedom. Descriptions of life there included reference to enjoyable general meetings, being able to learn a range of subjects, and the freedom to sew, knit, repair bikes and generally pursue interests regardless of gender. On leaving Summerhill, there could be difficulty initially in adapting to the strangeness of the outside world because of the viewpoints encountered (for example, negative attitudes towards women). This indicates the normative social construction of mainstream education. Nonetheless, adaptation was possible after some time. One former pupil taught himself to read in his twenties and now works in social enterprise. Another completed a PhD in education. Another worked for the BBC, although having no formal qualifications. The role of the learners was to pursue their interests. As they grew older, responsibility was encouraged; there was a requirement to clean their rooms and to do their washing. Lucas, the author, comments on the characteristics developed by the school—a lack of fear of failure, authority, social ostracism, or life. It is the kind of education that is probably only possible in smaller schools and where there is acceptance of risk as well as faith in development above qualifications.

It is not inconceivable that education could allow more freedom, but there would need to be some radical changes to thinking about learning, to the dependence on grades as a measure of success, and to the structure of free education (for example, reducing the length of full-time, free education) so that it could be an affordable approach. Other changes might include a radical alteration of the inspection system, or conducting no inspections at all, as is the case in Finland where teachers work together to improve teaching and learning so that a culture of "diversity, trust and respect" underpins the education system (Sahlberg, 2011: 127). The result is that teachers have greater responsibility than accountability and education professionals provide leadership rather than governance. If that seems like an impossible dream for the United Kingdom, it could reflect the constructed belief system of the reader who has been educated to think otherwise, a sign of the cynicism Sahlberg refers to: "Although the pursuit of transparency and accountability provides parents and politicians with more information, it also builds suspicion, low morale, and professional cynicism" (ibid.).

The kind of autonomy that might be possible in relation to education will not be independent of the conditions in which it is invoked. With reference to Foucault, Marshall (1996: 165) describes the 'autos' (self) as "contaminated by the nomos" (external laws). The autonomous self is relational and not independent; otherwise acting independently would be a random act that is unconnected to other people. The meaning of autonomy, much valued in liberal societies (Bottery, 2000), can lead to an individualism that ignores the effects, positive or negative, on others both locally and globally. Perhaps Foucault's view is justified that power relations are inherent in educational institutions, "which make us governable by masking the reality that our identities are being constituted" (Marshall, 1996: 216). That does not mean that nothing can be done to address tensions and inequalities, just that one can never get away completely from the effects of some form of dominance and social construction of who we are, who we might be, and how free we think we are to do it. The following comment by Foucault is quoted often:

> My point is not that everything is bad, but that everything is dangerous, which is not exactly the same as bad. If everything is dangerous, then we always have something to do. So my position leads not to apathy but to a hyper- and pessimistic activism. I think that the ethico-political choice we have to make every day is to determine which is the main danger. (1997: 117).

One danger at the moment is that emphasising learning for work in a teetering economy detracts from the opportunity for the kind of education that would be beneficial to both individuals and society. I am not convinced by the economic arguments that abound for altering education. Learning to develop one's interests and being encouraged to consider those that may seem alien to one's limited experience is not the same as learning for work or for the economy, although it could serve that purpose.

Vocational and Academic Pathways

One 'choice' that is made in education is between vocational and academic routes. Ostensibly, the choice is made during secondary education, but in practice there is a more limited choice of destiny. Such a destiny may be imagined by families prenatally or even preconception and will inform parenting from the outset. Teachers' roles as assessors, attributors and advisers are influential in this process, too.

Vocational education has become associated with training rather than education and courses that lead more directly to a job. It is not clearly defined, however, as was pointed out in *The Wolf Report* (2011). Examples of vocational subjects would be catering, construction, hairdressing, child care, business studies and engineering. The contents of the courses, however, are very likely to contain information that falls under the 'academic' heading, such as English, maths, physics and psychology. *Vocation* derives from the Latin for *calling* and is used to express the idea that particular types of work draw the interest of individuals. In the past, vocations were medicine, law and the clergy, occupations which require the study of 'academic' subjects and which could lead to a variety of courses or jobs.

One of the problems with learning in classrooms, which most schooling consists of, is that it is more compatible with learning that involves reading, thinking and writing than practical learning. An associated difficulty is devising a curriculum to meet certain demands for qualifications. For instance, cooking has become food technology and includes a written paper at GCSE in England, Wales and Northern Ireland. The practical element is only part of the assessment. It is not that the content of specifications is irrelevant but rather that the level of detail of what must be covered emphasises theory above practical and technical knowledge. Interest in the theory could arise spontaneously out of practice rather than being force-fed. However, this would require highly expert teachers, more consistent use of practical learning spaces, and different forms of assessment. Introducing compulsory academic elements into more practical subjects may be intended to raise their status but tends to detract from learners' intrinsic motivation to learn. The constraints on teachers can "make learning unpleasant, depressing, grey, unerotic" as Foucault says (1974, cited in Marshall, 1996: 7). Foucault goes on to suggest that this maintains power in society—"you have to make learning rebarbative [repellent] if you want to restrict the number of people who have access to knowledge" (ibid.).

The division between vocational and academic learning is socially divisive and epistemologically unjustified. It is a legacy of the tripartite system of education in the United Kingdom, which still lurks between and within educational establishments. The Butler Act proposed grammar schools, technical schools and secondary moderns after a general primary education. The type of knowledge to be acquired differed in each. Respectively these were intellectual, scientific and technical, and practical. Categorisation of knowledge can be found in Aristotle's writings from the fourth century BCE; *episteme* (knowledge) includes the distinction between *theoria* (similar to academic) and practical knowledge or *techné* (similar to technical and practical). *Episteme* is only one form of knowledge, the more general kind being *gnosis*. A fuller description of the types of knowledge and their relation to work-based learning can be found in Gibbs (2013).

Separating the type of knowledge required for different activities has led to an unnatural division between 'thinking' and 'doing' and, more worryingly, 'thinkers' and 'doers'. The idea that some individuals are better suited to certain kinds of education has a long history. Plato divided society into those men (*sic*) of gold, silver, bronze and iron, with each category suited to a particular occupation and way of life. Occasionally, Plato says, rather than a child resembling its parents, it may have "bronze or iron in its make-up, then they must harden their hearts, and degrade it to the ranks of the industrial and agricultural class where it properly belongs" (Boyd, 1962: 415). The UK education system retains different classes of education (academic, vocational, and technical), although attempts have been made to make the value of these more equal.

Teachers are likely to assign, consciously or less consciously, their learners to particular categories. Furthermore, the value of different pathways may be deliberately or inadvertently communicated. It has been suggested that teachers, most of whom have experienced higher education, "undervalue the world of industry and commerce and present a somewhat disparaging picture of this world in the classroom" (Elliott et al., 1980: 137). However, since that was written, there has been an increase in the importance of business and economics, with many young people studying the subjects at school, college and university. In addition, the increase in the number of learners, as participation rates have risen, has required more teachers of vocational subjects, who may be dual professionals (having expertise and an identity as both a teacher and an occupational specialist—see, e.g., Robson, 1998; Lingfield, 2012). This is not to say that categorisation and promotion of pathways does not take place but merely that what is disparaged may have changed.

There have been attempts to raise the status of vocational subjects and training. Some of these have been hampered by changes in government that result in new policies, with the result that reforms are either abandoned or altered. Choice of subjects and pathways is influenced by class, race and gender, thereby limiting choice. Tomlinson (2001) refers to the fear of middle-class parents that their offspring would be relegated to vocational education. The association between social status and type of employment runs deep. Lumby and Foskett (2005: 71) make this point:

> Choosing between academic and vocational pathways must be seen, therefore, as choosing to be defined as part of a particular social group, which will work its way out in terms of pathways, expectations and likely achievements throughout the rest of the individual's life.

One way to raise the status of different educational routes is to change the name so that vocational courses sound more academic (Green et al., 1999). *Food technology* rather than *cookery* is one example. Another example is *Curriculum 2000*, introduced in that year in England, Wales and Northern Ireland for post-16 study. It included a new AVCE (Advanced Vocational Certificate of Education) that mirrored the grading of A-levels and also included the word *advanced*. This gave way in England to a more radical suggestion that there should be an overarching diploma. The then-Labour government expressed some reluctance to accept the reform as proposed by Tomlinson (2004), demonstrated by parliamentary debate over the decision to retain an academic-vocational divide. Alan Johnson (education secretary at the time, quoted in the House of Commons

Education and Skills Committee report, 2006–7: 74) was concerned about the loss of the 'gold standard' A-level and diversity of qualifications, although how snobbery would be reduced was unclear:

> [Subsuming A-levels, GCSEs, and apprenticeships into a diploma] would be a mistake . . . This is what we are committed to do here to remove this very English snobbery. Let us leave Scotland Wales and Northern Ireland out of this. It is an English snobbery about academic qualifications being somehow infinitely superior to vocational qualifications.

Raising the status of vocational education is referred to as 'the German approach'. The French approach has been to broaden academic courses. The introduction of National Vocational Qualifications is an example of the former and Curriculum 2000 and diplomas an example of the latter. Neither of these solutions have been successful in England (Lumby & Foskett, 2007). Recent changes by the coalition government in England include the introduction of the EBacc (a measure of which subjects are taken, not a qualification—the "correct subjects" being English, maths, history or geography, the sciences and a language [Department for Education, 2014c]), changes to the grading for GCSEs, and a return to linear, rather than modular, A-level exams. What these changes will do is almost certainly raise the already-high status of academic courses, thereby ensuring that the tensions and inequalities around choice of subjects and pathway remain unresolved.

Equality and Equity

One question here is how fair an education system is in managing inevitable and valuable differences between people. It is unfortunate that there is a propensity to view difference in terms of what is better or worse. Humans are prone to categorisation and indeed are positively encouraged to do this in general and in formal education. The fact that one thing can be categorised as different from another, the basis of stereotyping, often leads to the next steps, prejudice (prejudging what someone is like) and discrimination (treating them differently because of that judgement).

One problem is that differential treatment is demanded in some cases and opposed in others. For example, 'differentiation' works on the principle of positive discrimination (or affirmative action), in which the different needs of learners are met. If it were a case of understanding what an individual knows already and finding ways to build on that knowledge, then that would seem less controversial than judging differences in learners based on assumptions about needs and backgrounds, which may not be at all accurate. It can also tempt teachers and learners down the pathway of excessive support and reducing challenge based on assumptions of capability associated with a category. This is just as true for those with specific learning needs as it is for any other learner in any institution. Teaching assistants may fall into this trap, for instance (see chapter five, Teachers).

The lecturer who blocked the request for help could be seen as avoiding any form of discrimination by applying the same principle to all students (assuming the response was a consistent one). However, equality of treatment is not necessarily appropriate, whereas an equal consideration of interests might be. For some time I have favoured an emphasis on inclusion above differentiation combined with high expectations for each person in terms of learning rather than performance goals. One can be sympathetic to the difficulties that learners experience without being drawn too far into compensatory strategies, which may lead to reduced independence and a sense of achievement (as a learning goal). What is essential, however, is to assist the learner with finding an alternative strategy or offering sufficient assistance to reinstate confidence. It is a difficult balance at times, one that requires negotiation above refusal or giving in. Learning becomes a joint responsibility under these circumstances. Teachers can be put under considerable pressure to ensure learners are successful, because they may be held accountable for poor results, because they care about their learners' futures, or because learners who pay fees for courses may believe they are entitled to success.

In the introductory chapter I referred to all students being given a distinction (although undeserved). This is another example of equality of treatment. Another form of equality is that of consideration of interest (Peczenik & Karlsson, 1995). If a teacher refuses to help any student, then that equates to equality of treatment, but that would not take into account consideration of interest because it cannot be assumed that all students are equally able to help themselves. This would make refusal inequitable.

> There is general agreement that the aim of public policy cannot and should not be equality in the sense that everyone is the same or achieves the same outcomes—a state that appears to be both impossible and undesirable. Rather, a commitment to equity suggests that differences in outcomes should not be attributable to differences in areas such as wealth, income, power or possessions. (Levin, 2003: 5)

Reduced selection at age 11 in the form of state-maintained comprehensive schools was introduced to the United Kingdom in the 1950s, except in Northern Ireland, and offers an education that the majority receives: 95 per cent in Scotland, for example (Bryce & Humes, 2008). According to a range of research, the hope and perhaps expectation that such a system would lead to greater equality, social mobility, and social integration do not seem to have been fulfilled (Paterson, 2012). Divisions in society run deeper than the school one attends, one could conclude, or perhaps the partial comprehensive system is implicated. How civic-minded and thus integrated people were, according to Paterson's longitudinal analysis of over 12,000 individuals, was mediated by cognitive ability, although that is partly mediated by cultural capital. The difficulty lies not so much in differences between who can do what but in the value associated with certain social roles or jobs, both in terms of status and earning potential.

The enormous challenge for the government is to reduce or remove the barriers imposed by material difference, which may be associated with differences in gender, age, race, or any other category that can be thought of. The assumption is often made in political rhetoric that education is the solution to inequity rather than taking into account the way education policy maintains difference and the need for wider policies to counteract inequitable differences. Meanwhile, a significant tension exists between (purportedly) embracing diversity and striving for social cohesion (Bell & Stevenson, 2006). Very recently (the spring of 2014) there has been a furore over an anonymous letter that claimed Islamic fundamentalists were plotting to take over schools in Birmingham (England)—likened to the Trojan horse. This led to 21 schools, all publicly funded and none faith schools, being inspected between March and May 2014. The chief inspector published an advice note to the government following the inspections that highlighted the inappropriate or weak role of governors (Wilshaw, 2014). At about the same time a row erupted between the home secretary, Theresa May, and the former secretary for education, Michael Gove, each suggesting the other was to blame for, respectively, not tackling extremism through immigration policy or following up concerns sooner. Having created a system in England in which schools can operate more freely and beyond local-authority control, it should not be surprising that such situations arise, whatever the truth of the allegations, underpinned as they are by society's divisions and suspicions.

Concluding Comments

Successive governments in the United Kingdom are responsible for the kind of education system that has developed. In spite of some differences, there is much that is shared. Nonetheless education is dominated by "the big kid on the block", England (Croxford, 2011). The extensive role of governance and its associated agencies in each region of the United Kingdom in deciding what education should look like also renders them responsible for the experience of those involved in putting policy into action as well as the experience of and outcomes for teachers and learners. Although they can be held to account at election time, it tends to be institutions, and sometimes parents, that are seen as the cause of different outcomes for learners. In England in particular, successive governments have made some larger and some smaller changes to education. It has been a very unsettling time for managers, teachers, learners and parents for a number of years.

Policy changes take time to settle and for consequences to unfold, often in unpredictable ways. There have been so many changes of late in England that it is impossible to be sure what the longer-term effects of previous policy would have been. Perhaps education should be taken out of the hands of the government. Scotland has an executive agency (Education Scotland) that deals with quality and improvement, providing some distance between central government and education. However, a better option might be to have a not-for-profit, all-party organisation that is responsible for education, one that does not make changes for political purposes or financial gain. Education should no longer be simply definable as 'politics'.

A review of the entire education system could be undertaken to begin with, including the many arbitrary aspects within it, such as the age at which learners move from one institution to the next. Very often, particular segments are reviewed and researched with different personnel (ministers, governors, teachers, academics, and researchers) holding an interest or expertise primarily in one aspect—for instance, early years or higher education—thereby losing a more comprehensive and longitudinal understanding. Parents, learners and other 'stakeholders' should be consulted across the United Kingdom in a review of any kind. Tensions and inequalities in the systems should be investigated with a view to finding ways to combat them without creating additional ones. To this end, regulation of the system is essential. Inevitably there will be compromise, but some common values might be established. The system or systems need a different kind of organisation based on a "clear specification and regulation of the roles, rights and responsibilities of the different parties" (Green et al, 1999: 256).

As long as formal education remains to a greater or lesser extent the responsibility of central governments, there needs to be much more precise use of terms such as *rights, choice, responsibility* and *autonomy*. It has become popular of late for politicians interviewed on the radio to open a sentence with 'Let's be clear', when what follows is far from clear. Education is not a clear matter. It is complex, untidy, expensive, socially divisive and time-consuming. For some it can be a source of inspiration, friendship and a relatively secure future. For others it is a source of stress and alienation. Freedom to learn should be the core business of a formal education system that is separated from party-political aims. Perhaps, as Einstein suggested, "There is too much education altogether" (Einstein, 1954: 57) and he was right when he said that education in the form of schooling stands in the way of learning. I would say that learning does take place but much of it involves the hidden curriculum. Dorling (2010) reminds us that the social evils of the twentieth century—ignorance, want, idleness, squalor and disease—have largely been replaced by five others: elitism, exclusion, prejudice, greed and despair. He says that, not least in England, "as those with most power continue to promote elitism, exclusion, prejudice, greed and despair, injustice will not be reduced" (ibid.: 4).

Chapter Summary

This final chapter has revisited important themes addressed in the previous chapters. The preface by Paddy McQueen develops the theme of recognition and its relevance to tensions and inequalities in the education system. The other themes included in the chapter are responsibility, autonomy, accountability and choice; the unnecessary divisiveness of vocational and academic pathways; and the tension between equality and equity. The meaning of responsibility is discussed because it has considerable implications for intersubjective constructions of teacher and student identity, as well as for achievement and progression. The meaning of autonomy is considered in relation to liberal ideology, and the section draws out some of the difficulties in promoting greater freedom whilst maintaining standards and preferred values. One underlying tension that has a long history and looks set to remain is the distinction between vocational and academic learning. Solutions include different ways to raise the status of vocational education, although that does not resolve the unhelpful binary that can lead to separating thinkers from doers. Some ideas for altering the education system are offered, in the hope that education could be more equitable and more enjoyable and contribute to a more equal society. Education in the United Kingdom is only one means to this end and should not be expected to be a cure-all for society's discontents. Finally, it is proposed that formal education requires regulation for equitable purposes, a process that should be separated from party politics.

APPENDIX

Education Provision in the United Kingdom

(E=England, NI=Northern Ireland, S=Scotland, W=Wales)

Table A.1 State-maintained provision (publicly funded)

School type	Age range	Region	Notes
Preschool	3–5	All	
Primary or junior school	4/5–11	All	Scottish islands 5–14
Secondary/high/community school (comprehensive, i.e., nonselective)	11–16	All	From 12 in Scotland. May be called an academy in Scotland. Some schools have retained *grammar* in the name although comprehensive.
Middle school	varies	E, W, NI	Limited number. Ages vary but in the range of 8–14.
Grammar school	11–16 or 19	E, NI	Selective intake. Ability test taken for entry.
Foundation school (trust school)	5–11/11–16	E, W, NI	Governors have more control than in a community school.
Voluntary maintained/aided	5–11/11–16	E, W, NI	Faith schools run by governors.

(continued)

Table A.1 *(Continued)*

School type	Age range	Region	Notes
Voluntary non-maintained/controlled	5–11/11–16	All	Faith schools run by local authority.
Integrated	5–11/11–16	NI	Non-faith schools. Diversity valued.
Irish medium schools/units	5–11/11–16	NI	
Gaelic medium schools	See notes	S	Some primary schools and one secondary. Gaelic medium used in some other schools and colleges.
Welsh medium schools	5–11/11–16	W	
Academies		E	Often formed from underperforming state schools.
Academy converters	11–16	E	Usually high-performing schools that are given greater autonomy.
Free schools—a type of (E) academy	Early years, primary, secondary, sixth form	E	Can be set up by community groups—e.g., teachers, parents.
Special schools	5–16	All	For learners with additional learning needs. Includes hospital schools.
Pupil referral units	5–16	All	Provide education for those who cannot stay in mainstream education for a variety of reasons—e.g., due to behavioural difficulties or being a victim of bullying.
Colleges of further education Further education	14 or 16–19 All ages	All	Further education is any study that is not higher education (can include work-based and adult education).

(continued)

School type	Age range	Region	Notes
City technology colleges	11–16/16–19	E	Urban schools specialising in technical subjects. Funded by businesses and central government.
University technical colleges	14–16, 16–19	E	Government funded. Specialise in technology and science.
Sixth form colleges	16–19	E, W, NI	
Sixth forms in schools	16–19	All	
Co-operative schools and colleges	3–19	All	Note that in England co-ops can be autonomous like academies (above). The rest of the United Kingdom has schools run on cooperative principles.
University (higher education)	18+	All	Very rarely younger students are accepted. The amount of public funding has reduced greatly. There are some maintenance grants. Otherwise funding is through a loan.

Table A.2 Fee-paid provision

School type	Age range	Region	Notes
Nursery	3–5	All	
Pre-preparatory (pre-prep) school	3–8	All	
Preparatory (prep) school	8–13	All	
Private school	Varies	All	A general term for a fee-paid school. Can be primary, secondary, or sixth form.

(continued)

Table A.2 *(Continued)*

School type	Age range	Region	Notes
Independent school	Varies	All	A general term for a fee-paid school. Can be primary, secondary, or sixth form.
Boarding school	Varies	All	Accommodation for students is provided either on a weekly or termly basis.
Public school	13–18	Mostly E	The term refers to some older, prestigious schools. They are usually boarding schools.
International school	Varies	All	Usually students are from countries other than the host one.
University	18+	E	Three exist at the moment.
Special schools	5–16	All	For learners with additional learning needs.

Table A.3 Qualifications

Region		Notes
Wales	Essential Skills Wales and Wider Key Skills	Under review. Essential Skills (communication, number, and digital literacy) recommended for adults. Both skill sets to be integrated in 14–16 education.
	GCSE	General Certificate in Secondary Education. Main qualification for 14–19.
	AS and A-level	Advanced Subsidiary and Advanced. Main qualification for 16–19.
	Welsh Baccalaureate	Available 14–19. Includes academic or vocational skills through four challenges (individual project, global citizenship, enterprise and employability, and community).

(continued)

Region		Notes
Scotland	QCF	Qualifications and Credit Framework at award, certificate, and diploma level for a range of vocational subjects and functional skills.
	IVA	International Vocational Award (four options, including police management and hydrocarbon process operations).
	National	Access. Intermediate (the equivalent of GCSEs; pass grades A to C).
	Higher	(equivalent to A-levels; pass grades A to C)
	HNC and HND	Higher National Certificate or Higher National Diploma. Work-related. Equivalent to degree level.
	Advanced Higher Scottish Baccalaureate	Higher and Advanced Higher (AH) courses combined into a coherent set (languages, science, expressive arts, or social sciences). Includes an interdisciplinary project at AH level.
Northern Ireland	NVQs	National Vocational Qualifications. Recognised by industry.
	Entry level	No entry requirements. Aim to develop skills in a range of subjects.
	Key Skills	Similar to Essential Skills (see Wales).
	GCSE	
	AS and A-level	
	BTECs	(Business and Technology Education Council.) Work-related qualifications taken either as well as or instead of A-levels.
	HNC and HND	
England	Functional Skills	Initial qualifications at Entry Level and in English, ICT, and Maths.
	NVQs	

(continued)

Table A.3 *(Continued)*

Region		Notes
	Entry level	
	Key Skills	
	GCSE	Plan to replace grading from A* to G with nine to one.
	AS and A-level	
	BTECs	
	HNC and HND	
All	Degree Diplomas	Examples: Undergraduate 'bachelor' awards, BA, BSc, BMus, BEd (primary, secondary), medical degrees (Scottish degrees take four years rather than three as elsewhere), postgraduate master's, MA, MSc, MEd PhD, EdD, and PGCE.

References

Academies Act (2010). Chapter 32. Accessed online October 28, 2013. http://www.legislation.gov.uk/ukpga/2010/32/pdfs/ukpga_20100032_en.pdf

Ahlberg, J. & A. Ahlberg (1990). *Starting School.* London: Puffin.

Alexander, W. P. (1946). *The Education Act: A Parent's Guide.* London: Phoenix House Limited.

Baby Signing Time! Accessed online July 18, 2012. http://www.babysigningtime.com/

Alldred, P. and M. E. David (2007). *Get Real about Sex: The Politics and Practice of Sex Education.* Maidenhead: McGraw Hill and Open University Press.

Altrichter, H. (2010). "Theory and Evidence on Governance: Conceptual and Empirical Strategies of Research on Governance in Education." *European Educational Research Journal.* 9 (2), 147–58.

Apprenticeship, Skills, Children and Learning Act (2009). London: Crown.

Aspin, D. N. & J. D. Chapman (2007). "Lifelong Learning: Concepts and Conceptions." In D. N. Aspin (ed.), *Philosophical Perspectives on Lifelong Learning.* Dordrecht: Springer, 19–38.

ATL (Association of Teachers and Lecturers). Accessed online December 30, 2013. http://www.atl.org.uk/

ATL (2013). "Teaching on the Cheap is Selling Children Short: Schools Use Teaching Assistants and Cover Supervisors to Teach Children." Accessed online January 1, 2014. http://www.atl.org.uk/media-office/media-archive/teaching-on-cheap-teaching-assistants.asp

Audit Scotland (2012). "Scotland's Colleges: Current Finances, Future Challenges." Edinburgh: Audit Scotland.

Badley, G., & T. Habeshaw (1991). "The Changing Role of the Teacher in Higher Education." *British Journal of In-Service Education.* 17 (3), 212–18.

Ball, S. J. (2003). *Class Strategies and the Education Market: The Middle Classes and Social Advantage*. Abingdon: RoutledgeFalmer.

Ball, S. J. (2008, 2013). *The Education Debate*. Bristol: The Policy Press.

Ball, S. J. and C. Junemann (2012). *Networks, New Governance and Education*. Bristol: Policy Press.

Ball, S. J., M. Maguire, & A. Braun with K. Hoskins & J. Perryman (2012). *How Schools Do Policy: Policy Enactments in Secondary Schools*. London: Routledge.

Ball, S. J., M. Maguire, & S. Macrae (2000). "'Worlds apart'—Education Markets in the Post-16 Sector of One Urban Locale." In F. Coffield, *Differing Visions of a Learning Society: Research Findings; Volume 1*. Bristol: The Policy Press, 39–70.

Barber, M. (1994). *The Making of the 1944 Education Act*. London: Cassell Education.

Barnett, R. (2008). "Critical Professionalism in an Age of Supercomplexity." In B. Cunningham (ed.), *Exploring Professionalism*. London: Bedford Way Papers, 190–207.

BBC (2014). "Parents' Group Calls for More School Inspections." Accessed online January 16, 2014. http://www.bbc.co.uk/democracylive/northern-ireland-25656243

BBC News (October 10, 2013). "University Boss: Headteacher, Mayor or Chief Executive?" Accessed online October 28, 2013. http://www.bbc.co.uk/news/education-24462298

BBC News (October 15, 2013). "Gove Urged to Monitor Free Schools 'More Closely.'" Accessed online November 8, 2013. http://www.bbc.co.uk/news/education-24539353

BBC News (December 1, 2013). "Osborne Distances Himself from Boris Johnson over IQ Comments." Accessed online January 4, 2013. http://www.bbc.co.uk/news/uk-politics-25175817

BBC News (January 26, 2014). "Sir Michael Wilshaw 'Spitting Blood' over Ofsted Attack." Accessed online March 2, 2014. http://www.bbc.co.uk/news/education-25900547

BBC News (February 12, 2014). "Wilshaw 'Urged Gove Not to Drop Ofsted Chairwoman.'" Accessed online March 2, 2014. http://www.bbc.co.uk/news/education-26151572

Becoming a School Governor (2013–2014). DENI. Accessed online October 11, 2013. http://www.deni.gov.uk/becoming_a_school_governor_booklet.pdf

Bell, L. & H. Stevenson (2006). *Education Policy: Process, Themes and Impact*. Routledge, London.

Benn, M. (2013). *What Should We Tell Our Daughters? The Pleasures and Pressures of Growing Up Female.* London: John Murray.

Bennis, W. (2009). *On Becoming a Leader.* New York: Basic Books.

Berlin, I. (1969). *Four Essays on Liberty.* Oxford: Oxford University Press.

Berman, G. & A. Dar (2013). *Prison Population Statistics.* House of Commons Library. Standard Note: SN/SG/4334. Accessed online September 8, 2013. www.parliament.uk/briefing-papers/sn04334.pdf

Bernstein, B. (1961). "Social Structure, Language and Learning." *Education Research.* 3 (3), 163–76.

Berry, A. (2007). *Tensions in Teaching about Teaching: Understanding Practice as a Teacher Educator.* Dordrecht: Springer.

BHA (2012). "'Faith Ethos' Academies and Free Schools explained." Briefing from the British Humanist Association. http://humanism.org.uk/wp-content/uploads/bha-briefing-faith-ethos-academies-and-free-schools-explained.pdf

Bierema, L. L. & M. Eraut (2004). "Workplace-Focused Learning: Perspective on Continuing Professional Education and Human Resource Development." *Advances in Developing Human Resources.* 6 (1), 52–68.

Biggs, J. B. & C. Tang (2011). *Teaching for Quality Learning at University.* 4th edition. Maidenhead: Open University Press.

BIS (2012). "Consultation on Revocation of the Further Education Workforce Regulations, Government Response." London: Crown (Department for Business, Innovation & Skills).

Bivins, T. (2006). "Responsibility and Accountability." In K. Fitzpatrick & C. Bronstein (eds.), *Ethics in Public Relations: Responsible Advocacy.* Thousand Oaks, CA: Sage Publications, 19–39.

Blenkinsop, S., T. McCrone, P. Wade, & M. Morris (2006). "How Do Young People Make Choices at 14 and 16?" Annesley: DfES Publications.

Bottery, M. (2000). *Education Policy and Ethics.* London: Continuum.

Bourdieu, P. & J.-C. Passeron (1977). *Reproduction in Education, Society and Culture.* London: Sage Publications Ltd.

Bourdieu, P. (1986). "The Forms of Capital." In J. Richardson (ed.), *Handbook of Theory and Research for the Sociology of Education.* New York: Greenwood, 241–58.

Boyd, W. (1962). *Plato's Republic for Today.* London: Heinemann.

Bridge Schools Trust. Accessed online October 3, 2013. http://www.bridgeschoolsinspectorate.co.uk/home

Broad, J. (2006). "Interpretations of Independent Learning in Further Education." *Journal of Further and Higher Education.* 30 (2), 119–43.

Broadfoot, P. & M. Osborn with M. Gilly & A. Paillet (1995). "What Professional Responsibility Means to Teachers: National Contexts and Classroom Constants." In L. Dawtrey, J. Holland, M. Hammer, & S. Sheldon (eds.), *Equality and Inequality in Education Policy.* Clevedon: Open University Press, 221–41.

Brophy, J. E. (1982). "Research on the Self-Fulfilling Prophecy and Teacher Expectations." Michigan: The Institute for Research on Teaching.

Brown, P. (1994). "Education and the Ideology of Parentocracy." In M. J. Halstead (ed.), *Parental Choice and Education: Principles, Policy and Practice.* London: Kogan Page Ltd., 51–67.

Bryce, T. G. K. & W. M. Humes (2008). "Secondary Education: Philosophy and Practice." In T. G. K. Bryce & W. M. Humes, *Scottish Education: Third Edition Beyond Devolution.* Edinburgh: Edinburgh University Press, 33–46.

Burgess, S., E. Greaves, A. Vignoles, & D. Wilson (2009). "What Parents Want: School Preferences and School Choice." Working Paper No. 09/222. Accessed online January 15, 2014. http://www.bris.ac.uk/cmpo/publications/papers/2009/wp222.pdf

The Burgundy Book (2000). "Conditions of Service for School Teachers in England and Wales." Accessed online December 29, 2013. http://www.teachers.org.uk/files/active/0/Burgundy%20Book%20-%20July%2008%20-%20for%20Hearth.pdf

Burns, W. E. (2010). *A Brief History of Great Britain.* New York: Facts on File.

Butler, E. (2013). *Foundations of a Free Society.* London: The Institute of Economic Affairs.

Butler, N. M. (1915). *The Meaning of Education: Contributions to a Philosophy of Education.* New York: Scribner.

Caddell, D., J. Crowther, P. O'Hara, & L. Tett (2000). "Investigating the Roles of Parents and Schools in Children's Early Years Education." Paper presented at the European Conference on Educational Research, Edinburgh, September 20–23, 2000. Accessed online July 18, 2012. http://www.leeds.ac.uk/educol/documents/00001660.htm

Cameron, David (March 7, 2013). "Economy Speech." Accessed online September 20, 2013. https://www.gov.uk/government/speeches/economy-speech-delivered-by-david-cameron

Campbell, C. (2005). *The Romantic Ethic and the Spirit of Modern Consumerism.* 3rd edition. York: Alcuin Academics.

Cardiff Council (2013). "Report of County Clerk and Monitoring Officer: Establishment of a New Shadow Governing Body and Appointment of Local Authority School Governor." Accessed online October 29, 2013. www.cardiff.gov.uk/objview.asp?object_id=27368

Carter-Wall, C. & G. Whitfield (2012). 'The Role of Aspirations, Attitudes and Behaviour in Closing the Educational Attainment Gap." York: Joseph Rowntree Foundation.

CAVTL (2013). "It's About Work . . . Excellent Adult Vocational Teaching and Learning." Learning and Skills Improvement Service. Accessed online December 31, 2013. http://www.excellencegateway.org.uk/cavtl

Children & Young People Now (2010). "Government Clarifies Ban on Every Child Matters." Accessed online January 3, 2014. http://www.cypnow.co.uk/cyp/news/1053008/government-clarifies-ban-every-child-matters

Children's Act (1989). Accessed online July 10, 2012. http://www.legislation.gov.uk/ukpga/1989/41/contents

The Children's Society (2013). "Supporting Pupils Who Are Young Carers: Information for Teachers and School Staff." Colden Common: The Children's Society.

Chowen, S. (ed.) (2013). *Should Teaching Qualifications Be Left to Chance?* London: Institute for Learning.

Claxton, G., M. Chambers, G. Powell, & B. Lucas (2011). *The Learning Powered School.* Bristol: TLO Limited.

Cleaver, H., I. Unell, & J. Aldgate (2011). *Children's Needs—Parenting Capacity: Child abuse; Parental Mental Illness, Learning Disability, Substance Misuse, and Domestic Violence.* 2nd edition. London: The Stationery Office.

Code of Professionalism and Conduct (2012). Edinburgh: General Teaching Council for Scotland.

Code of Values and Professional Practice in Northern Ireland (2004). Accessed online August 14, 2013. http://www.gtcni.org.uk/uploads/docs/GTC_code.pdf

Coe, R., K. Jones, J. Searle, D. Kokotsaki, A. M. Kosnin, & P. Skinner (2008). "Evidence on the Effects of Selective Educational Systems: A Report for the Sutton Trust." Durham: CEM Centre. Accessed online April 8, 2014. http://www.suttontrust.com/public/documents/SuttonTrustFullReportFinal1.pdf

Coffield, F., C. Costa, W. Muller, & J. Webber (2014). *Beyond Bulimic Learning: Improving Teaching in Further Education.* London: Institute of Education.

Colebatch, H. K. (2006). "Thinking about Policy: Finding the Best Way." Paper presented at GovNet International Conference, Australian National University, November 29–December 1, 2006.

Colley, H., D. James, M. Tedder, & K. Diment (2004). "Learning as Becoming in Vocational Education and Training: Class, Gender and the Role of Vocational Habitus." *Journal of Vocational Education and Training*. 55 (4), 471–98.

Committee for Employment and Learning (2013). "Official Report (Hansard)." June 26. Accessed online December 31, 2013. http://www.niassembly.gov.uk/Assembly-Business/Official-Report/Committee-Minutes-of-Evidence/Session-2012-2013/June-2013/General-Teaching-Council-for-Northern-Ireland--DELDE-Briefing-on-Proposed-Reform/

Committee of University Chairs (2009). *Guide for Members of Higher Education Governing Bodies in the UK*. Accessed online October 11, 2013. http://www.hefce.ac.uk/media/hefce1/pubs/hefce/2009/0914/09_14.pdf

Conly, S. (2013). *Against Autonomy: Justifying Coercive Paternalism*. Cambridge: Cambridge University Press.

The Conservative Government Quality of Life Manifesto (2010). "Modern Conservatism: Our Quality of Life Agenda." London: Conservative Party.

Conway, D. (2010) *Liberal Education and the National Curriculum*. London: Civitas.

Cook, W. (2013). "Vocational Education in English School: Protecting Options for Pre-16 Pupils." London: Institute for Public Policy Research.

Cotterall, S. (2000). "Promoting Learner Autonomy through the Curriculum: Principles for Designing Language Courses." *ELT Journal*. 54 (2), 109–17.

Coughlan, S. (2013). "Bail Out Universities Rather Than Banks?" BBC News. June 21, 2013. Accessed online March 22, 2014. http://www.bbc.co.uk/news/business-22756408

Creech, A., S. Hallam, M. Varvarigou, H. Gaunt, H. McQueen, & A. Pincas (2014). "The Role of Musical Possible Selves in Supporting Subjective Well-Being in Later Life." *Music Education Research*. 16 (1), 32–49.

Croxford, L. (2011). "School Systems across the UK." *Rise Review*. May 2011. Accessed online May 11, 2014. http://risetrust.org.uk/pdfs/Review_school-systems-may-2011.pdf

Crozier, G. & D. Reay (eds.) (2005). *Activating Participation: Parents and Teachers Working towards Partnership*. Stoke-on-Trent: Trentham Books.

Daily Mail online (2009). Accessed online January 30, 2014. http://www.dailymail.co.uk/news/article-1169534/Teen-tearaway-sent-public-school-ill-fated-television-experiment-proud-dad--high-hopes-daughter.html

David, M. E. (1980). *The State, the Family and Education*. London: Routledge.

David, M. E. (1993). *Parents, Gender and Education Reform*. Cambridge: Polity Press.

David, M. E., R. Edwards, M. Hughes, & J. Ribbens (1993). *Mothers and Education: Inside Out?; Exploring Family-Education Policy and Experience*. Basingstoke: Macmillan.

David, M. E., A. West, & J. Ribbens (1994). *Mother's Intuition? Choosing Secondary Schools*. London: Falmer Press.

Dawtrey, L., J. Holland, M. Hammer, & S. Sheldon (eds.) (1995). *Equality and Inequality in Education Policy*. Clevedon: Open University Press.

DCSF (2007). *Guidance on Education-Related Parenting Contracts, Parenting Orders and Penalty Notices*. Revised edition. Nottingham: DCSF Publications.

DENI (Audit 2012) (Department of Education). *Audit of Inequalities and Action Plan 2012–2015*. Accessed online November 19, 2013. http://www.deni.gov.uk/de1_12_7205__final_published_version_audit_of_inequalities_action_plan_june_2012.pdf

DENI. *Becoming a School Governor* (2013–14). Accessed online April 25, 2014. http://www.deni.gov.uk/becoming_a_school_governor_booklet.pdf

DENI (2008). *Guidance for Boards of Governors on the Formulation and Implementation of Salary Policy*. Accessed online December 18, 2013. http://www.deni.gov.uk/de1_12_92589__tnppt_-_guidance_for_boards_of_governors_on_the_formulation_and_implementation_of_salary_-_final_version.pdf

DENI (2012). "Department of Education Vision." Accessed online September 27, 2013. http://www.deni.gov.uk/index/about-the-department/department-of-education.htm

DENI (2013a). "Entitlement Framework." Accessed online November 17, 2013. http://www.deni.gov.uk/index/curriculum-and-learningt-new/curriculum-and-assessment-2/entitlement-framework.htm

DENI (2013b) "Integrated schools." Accessed online November 8, 2013. http://www.deni.gov.uk/index/schools-and-infrastructure-2/schools-management/10-types_of_school-nischools_pg/16-schools-integratedschools_pg.htm

Department for Education (no date). Accessed online September 19, 2013. https://www.gov.uk/government/organisations

Department for Education (2010). "The Importance of Teaching: The Schools White Paper." London: HMSO.

Department for Education (2011a). "Supporting Families in the Foundation Years." London: Crown.

Department for Education (2011b). "New Free Schools Are a Popular Choice for Parents." Accessed online July 12, 2012. http://www.education.gov.uk/inthenews/inthenews/a00197713/new-free-schools-are-a-popular-choice-for-parents-with-latest-analysis-showing-that-half-are-in-the-30-per-cent-most-deprived-communities

Department for Education (2011c). *Support and Aspiration: A New Approach to Special Educational Needs and Disability*. London: Crown.

Department for Education (2012a). "Prime Minister Announces Support for Families." May 18. Accessed online July 10, 2012. http://www.education.gov.uk/inthenews/inthenews/a00209164/pm-announces-family-support

Department for Education (2012b). "The Role of Parents in a Child's Learning." Accessed online July 10, 2012. http://www.education.gov.uk/childrenandyoungpeople/families/a00203160/role-of-parents-in-childs-learning

Department for Education (2012c). "Categories and Roles of School Governors." Accessed online July 23, 2012. http://www.education.gov.uk/schools/leadership/governance/becomingagovernor/rolesandresponsibilities/a0056694/categories-and-roles-of-school-governors

Department for Education (2012d). "Parent Governor Representatives." Accessed online January 15, 2014. http://www.education.gov.uk/schools/leadership/governance/a0014569/parent-governor-representatives

Department for Education (2012e). "Government Changes Definition of Persistent Absence to Deal with Reality of Pupil Absenteeism in Schools." Accessed online July 24, 2012. http://www.education.gov.uk/inthenews/inthenews/a00192057/government-changes-definition-of-persistent-absence-to-deal-with-reality-of-pupil-absenteeism-in-schools

Department for Education (2012f). *School Teachers' Pay and Conditions Document 2012 and Guidance on School Teachers' Pay and Conditions*. London: Crown.

Department for Education (2012g). *Behaviour and Discipline in Schools: A Guide for Head Teachers and School Staff*. London: Crown.

Department for Education (2013a). *Review of Efficiency in the Schools System*. London: Crown. DFE-00091-2013.

Department for Education (2013b). *Education and Training Statistics for the UK: 2012*. Tables 1 and 2. Accessed online January 6, 2013. https://www.gov.uk/government/publications/education-and-training-statistics-for-the-uk-2012

Department for Education (2013c). *Evidence to the STRB: The 2014 Pay Award*. London: Crown. DFE-00289-2013.

Department for Education (2014a). *Governors' Handbook: For Governors in Maintained Schools, Academies and Free Schools*. London: Crown.

Department for Education (2014b). "Health and Wellbeing: United Nations Convention on the Rights of the Child (UNCRC)." Accessed online March 8, 2014. http://www.education.gov.uk/childrenandyoungpeople/healthandwellbeing/b0074766/uncrc

Department for Education (2014c). "English Baccalaureate: Information for Schools." Accessed online April 8, 2014. https://www.gov.uk/english-baccalaureate-information-for-schools

Department for Employment and Learning (2008). "Guide for Governors of Further Education Colleges." Accessed online October 28, 2013. http://www.delni.gov.uk/guide_for_governors_fe_colleges_-_11_sept.pdf

Department of Education (1987). "Teachers' (Terms and Conditions of Employment) Regulations (Northern Ireland)." *Statutory Rules of Northern Ireland*. No. 267. London: Her Majesty's Stationery Office.

Devlin, B., M. Daniels, & K. Roeder (1997). "The Heritability of IQ." *Nature*. 388 (6,641), 468–71.

Devon County Council (2013). *Education Infrastructure Plan 2013–2031*. Accessed online November 8, 2013. http://www.devon.gov.uk/education-infrastructure-plan-v1.pdf

Directgov. "School Attendance and Absence: The Law." Accessed online July 23, 2012. http://www.direct.gov.uk/en/parents/schoolslearninganddevelopment/yourchildswelfareatschool/dg_066966

Dorling, D. (2010). *Injustice: Why Social Inequality Persists*. Bristol: The Policy Press.

Drennan, L. T. (2001). "Quality Assessment and the Tension between Teaching and Research." *Quality in Higher Education*. 7 (3), 167–78.

Duncan, G. & R. Murnane (eds.) (2011). *Whither Opportunity? Rising Inequality, Schools, and Children's Life Chances*. New York: Russell Sage Foundation.

Dweck, C. S. (1999). *Self Theories: Their Role in Motivation, Personality, and Development*. Hove: Psychology Press.

Earley, P., R. Nelson, R. Higham, S. Bubb, V. Porritt, & M. Coates (2011). *Experiences of New Headteachers in Cities*. Nottingham: National College for School Leadership.

Ecclestone, K. & D. Hayes (2009). *The Dangerous Rise of Therapeutic Education*. Abingdon, Routledge.

Education Act (2002). London: HMSO.

Education Committee (2010). "Examination of Witnesses (Question Numbers 60–72)." July 28, 2010. Accessed online January 3, 2014. http://www.publications.parliament.uk/pa/cm201011/cmselect/cmeduc/395-i/395-i05.htm

Education Scotland (no date). Accessed online August 9, 2013. http://www.educationscotland.gov.uk/thecurriculum/index.asp

Education Scotland (website, no date). "The Purpose of the Curriculum." Accessed online February 20, 2014. http://www.educationscotland.gov.uk/thecurriculum/whatiscurriculumforexcellence/thepurposeofthecurriculum/

Education Scotland (2012). *Framework Document*. Accessed online September 26, 2013. http://www.educationscotland.gov.uk/Images/EducationScotlandFrameworkDocument_tcm4-745890.pdf

Education Scotland (2014). "Roles and Responsibilities." Accessed online February 17, 2014. http://www.educationscotland.gov.uk/learningteachingandassessment/assessment/about/partnership/rolesandresponsibilities/learners.asp

Egan, D. (2013). *Poverty and Low Educational Achievement in Wales: Student, Family and Community Interventions*. York: Joseph Rowntree Foundation.

Einstein, A. (1954). *Ideas and Opinions*. New York: Crown Publishers, Inc.

Elias, J. L. & S. B. Merriam (1995). *Philosophical Foundations of Adult Education*. 2nd edition. Malabar, FL: Kreiger.

Elliott, J., D. Bridges, D. Ebbutt, R. Gibson, & J. Nias (1980). *School Accountability*. London: Grant McIntyre Ltd.

Emerson, G. B. *The Schoolmaster: The Proper Character, Studies, and Duties of the Teacher; Part 2*. In *The School and the Schoolmaster: A Manual* (1842). New York: Harper and Brothers.

"Enterprise Zones Wales" (2013). Accessed online October 9, 2013. http://wales.gov.uk/topics/businessandeconomy/help/enterprisezones/?lang=en

Equality Act (2010). London: Her Majesty's Stationery Office.

Equality Challenge Unit (2009). *The Experience of Black and Minority Ethnic Staff Working in Higher Education: Literature Review*. Accessed online January 7, 2013. http://www.mmu.ac.uk/equality-and-diversity/doc/experience-of-bme-staff-in-he.pdf

Equality and Human Rights Commission (2010). *Research Report 61: Significant Inequalities in Scotland; Identifying Significant Inequalities and Priorities for Action*. Manchester: Equality and Human Rights Commission.

Equality and Human Rights Commission (2010). *How Fair is Britain? Equality, Human Rights and Good Relations in 2010*. Accessed online March 7, 2014. http://www.equalityhumanrights.com/uploaded_files/triennial_review/how_fair_is_britain_-_complete_report.pdf

Equal Opportunities Commission (2007). *Valuable Assets: A General Formal Investigation into the Role and Status of Classroom Assistants in Scottish Schools*. Glasgow: Equal Opportunities Commission.

ETF (2014). http://www.et-foundation.co.uk/our-organisation/

Every Child Matters (2003). London: The Stationery Office.

Ericsson, K. A., R. T. Krampe, & C. Tesch-Romer (1993). "The Role of Deliberate Practice in the Acquisition of Expert Performance." *Psychological Review*. 100 (3), 363–406.

Estyn (2013). "The impact of teacher absence." Cardiff: Crown.

Evans, G. R. & J. Gill (2001). *Universities and Students: A Guide to Rights, Responsibilities and Practical Remedies*. London: Kogan Page Ltd.

Foucault, M. (1997). "What is Enlightenment?" In P. Rabinow (ed.), *The Essential Works of Foucault, 1954-1984, Volume 1: Ethics; Subjectivity and Truth*. New York: New Press.

Freeman, R. E. (2010). *Strategic Management: A Stakeholder Approach*. Cambridge: Cambridge University Press.

Freire, P. (1970). *Pedagogia del oprimido*. Mexico City: Siglo xxi editores.

Fromm, E. (1976, 2007). *To Have or to Be?* London: Continuum.

Fry, H., S. Ketteridge, & S. Marshall (2009). *A Handbook for Teaching and Learning in Higher Education: Enhancing Academic Practice*. 3rd edition. Abingdon, Oxon: Routledge.

Furedi, F. (2004). *Therapy Culture: Cultivating Vulnerability in an Uncertain Age*. London: Routledge.

Furedi, F. (2011). "Introduction to the Marketization of Higher Education and the Student as Consumer." In M. Molesworth, R. Scullion, & E. Nixon (eds.), *The Marketisation of Higher Education and the Student as Consumer*. Abingdon, Routledge, 1–7.

Further and Higher Education Act (1992). Chapter 13. London: The Stationery Office.

Gallagher and Smith (2000). "The Effects of the Selective System of Secondary Education in Northern Ireland." Accessed online December

12, 2013. http://www.deni.gov.uk/22ppa_gallagherandsmith_main-report.pdf

Garland, D. (1996). "The Limits of the Sovereign State." *British Journal of Criminology.* 36 (4), 445–71.

Garratt, D. & G. Forrester (2012). *Education Policy Unravelled.* London: Continuum International Publishing Group.

Gearon, L. (ed.) (2002). *Education in the United Kingdom: Structures and Organisation.* London: David Fulton Publishers.

Gibbs, P. (ed.). *Learning, Work and Practice: New Understandings.* Dordrecht: Springer.

Gibton, D. (2013). *Law, Education, Politics, Fairness: England's Extreme Legislation for Education Reform.* London: IoE Press.

Giddens, A. (ed.) (2001). *The Global Third Way Debate.* Cambridge: Polity Press.

Giesinger, J. (2012). "Respect in Education." *Journal of Philosophy of Education.* 46 (1): 100–12.

Gilbert, C. (2012). *Towards a Self-Improving System: The Role of School Accountability.* Nottingham: National College for School Leadership.

Gillborn, D. & H. Mirza (2000). *Inequality: Mapping Race, Class and Gender; A Synthesis of Research Evidence.* London: Office for Standards in Education.

Gillies, V. (2012). "Family Policy and the Politics of Parenting: From Function to Competence." In M. Richter & S. Andresen (eds.), *The Politicization of Parenthood: Shifting Private and Public Responsibilities in Education and Child Rearing.* London: Springer, 13–26.

Gilmore, S., J. Herring, & R. Probert (2009). "Introduction: Parental Responsibility—Law, Issues and Themes." In R. Probert, S. Gilmore, & J. Herring, *Responsible Parents and Parental Responsibility.* Oxford: Hart Publishing, 1–20.

Giroux, H. A. (2001). "Reproduction, Resistance, and Accommodation." In H. A. Giroux (ed.), *Theory and Resistance in Education: Towards a Pedagogy for the Opposition.* Westport: Bergin & Garvey, 72–111.

Gove, M. (2009). "What is Education for?" Speech to the RSA. June 30, 2009. Accessed online August 13, 2013. http://www.thersa.org/__data/assets/pdf_file/0009/213021/Gove-speech-to-RSA.pdf

Gove, M. (2010). "A Coalition for Good—How We Can All Work Together to Make Opportunity More Equal." Speech made at Brighton College, May 10, 2012. Accessed online November 17, 2013. https://www.gov.uk/government/speeches/education-secretary-michael-goves-speech-to-brighton-college

Gove, M. (2010). Letter to chief executives and directors of children's services. June 18. Accessed online July 12, 2012. http://www.education.gov.uk/schools/leadership/typesofschools/freeschools/b0061428/free-schools

Gove, M. (2012). Speech to the National College Annual Conference, Birmingham. June 16, 2010. Accessed online January 1, 2014. https://www.gov.uk/government/speeches/michael-gove-to-the-national-college-annual-conference-birmingham

Gove, M. (2013). Letter to Glenys Stacey, Ofqual. September 6. Accessed online February 20, 2014. http://ofqual.gov.uk/news/publication-notice/

Governors Wales (2013). "A Handbook for Governors of Schools in Wales: Part 1." Accessed online October 11, 2013. http://www.governorswales.org.uk/media/files/documents/2013-08-19/The_Role_of_a_School_Governor_English_1.pdf

Gravells, A. (2012). *Preparing to Teach in the Lifelong Learning Sector.* London: Learning Matters (Sage).

Green, A., A. Wolf, & T. Leney (1999). *Convergence and Divergence in European Education and Training Systems.* London: Institute of Education.

Griggs, R. (2012). *Report of the Review of Further Education Governance in Scotland.* Edinburgh: Crown.

The Guardian (2012). "The Trainee Teachers Who Are Paying to Work for Nothing." March 26. Accessed online January 1, 2014. http://www.theguardian.com/education/2012/mar/26/colleges-unpaid-trainee-lecturers

The Guardian Professional (2012). "Digital Technologies and the Tensions between Research and Teaching." April 18. Accessed online January 4, 2014. http://www.theguardian.com/higher-education-network/blog/2012/apr/18/digital-technologies-research-teaching

The Guardian (August 11, 2013). Accessed online August 12, 2013. http://www.theguardian.com/education/2013/aug/11/academy-schools-teachers-grade-inflation

The Guardian (2013). "Flagship Free School 'Misused Funds'". October 25. Accessed online December 12, 2013. http://www.theguardian.com/education/2013/oct/25/flagship-free-school-kings-science-academy

Hallam, S., A. Creech, H. Gaunt, A. Pincas, H. McQueen, & M. Varvarigou (2011). "Music for Life: Promoting Social Engagement and Wellbeing through Community Supported Participation in Musical Activities." London: Institute of Education.

Hammersley-Fletcher, L., M. Lowe, & J. Pugh (2006). *The Teaching Assistant's Guide.* Abingdon: Routledge.

Hansard (October 17, 2013). Accessed online October 29, 2013. http://www.publications.parliament.uk/pa/cm201314/cmhansrd/cm131017/debtext/131017-0001.htm

Hansen, K., H. Joshi, & S. Dex (2010). *Children of the 21st Century: The First Five Years*. Bristol: The Policy Press.

Hargreaves, D. H. (2012). *The Challenge for the Comprehensive School: Culture, Curriculum and Community.* Abingdon: Routledge. (First published 1982, London: Routledge & Kegan Paul Ltd.)

Harper, H. (2013). *Outstanding Teaching in Lifelong Learning*. Maidenhead: Open University Press.

Harris, N. (2009). "Playing Catch-Up in the Schoolyard? Children and Young People's 'Voice' and Education Rights in the UK." *International Journal of Law, Policy and the Family*. 23 (3), 331–66.

Harvard Committee (1945). *General Education in a Free Society: Report of the Harvard Committee with an Introduction by James Bryant Conant.* Cambridge: Harvard University Press.

Hattie, J. (2009). *Visible Learning: A Synthesis of over 800 Meta-Analyses Relating to Achievement*. Abingdon: Routledge.

Hawtry, S. (1870). "The Aim, the Duties, and the Reward of a Schoolmaster." Address delivered to the masters of St. Mark's School. November 10. London: Hamilton Adams & Co.

Hebb, D. O. (1955). "Drives and the C.N.S. (Conceptual Nervous System)." *The Psychological Review*. 62 (4), 243–54.

HEFCE (2013). "Student Satisfaction at a Nine-Year High." Higher Education Funding Council for England. Accessed online March 14, 2014. http://www.hefce.ac.uk/news/newsarchive/2013/news82928.html

Henricson, C. (2003). *Government and Parenting: Is There a Case for a Policy Review and a Parents' Code?* York: Joseph Rowntree Foundation.

HESA (Higher Education Statistics Agency). "Statistical First Release." HESA SFR 185. Accessed online January 6, 2014. http://www.hesa.ac.uk/index.php?option=com_content&task=view&id=2662&Itemid=161

Hill, R. (2013). *The Future Delivery of Education Services in Wales*. Accessed online October 9, 2013. http://wales.gov.uk/docs/dcells/consultation/130621-delivery-of-education-report-en.pdf

Hirsch, D. (2007). *Chicken and Egg: Child Poverty and Education Inequalities*. London: Child Poverty Action Group.

Holloway, S. & H. Pimlott-Wilson (2012). "Research Summary: Who Wants Parenting Classes and Why? The Primary Years." Centre for Research in Identity, Governance and Society. Accessed online July 24, 2012.

http://www.lboro.ac.uk/service/publicity/newsreleases/2012/94_Primary%20Parenting%20Classes%20Research%20Summary.pdf

Honneth, A. (1995). *The Struggle for Recognition: The Moral Grammar of Conflicts*. Cambridge: Polity.

Honneth, A. (2007). *Disrespect: The Normative Foundations of Critical Theory*. Cambridge: Polity.

Hood, S. (1999). "Home-school Agreements: A True Partnership?" *School Leadership & Management*. 19 (4), 427–40.

Hopkins, D. (2003). "Understanding Networks for Innovation in Policy and Practice." In *Networks of Innovation: Towards New Models for Managing Schools and Systems*. Paris: OECD, 153–63.

House of Commons Education and Skills Committee (2007). *14-19 Diplomas: Fifth Report of Session 2006–07*. London: The Stationery Office.

Hoyle, E. (1969). *The Role of the Teacher*. London: Routledge & Kegan Paul.

Hoyle, E (1974). "Professionality, Professionalism and Control in Teaching," *London Educational Review*. 3 (2), 13–19.

Hoyle, E. (2008). "Changing Conceptions of Teaching as a Profession." In D. Johnson and R. Maclean (eds.), *Teaching: Professionalization, Development and Leadership*. New York: Springer, 285–304.

Hoyle, E. & M. Wallace (2005). *Educational Leadership: Ambiguities, Professionals & Managerialism*. London: Sage Publications Ltd.

Hsieh, Y.-C. (2012). "Shaping Young People's Gender and Sexual Identities: Can Teaching Practices Produce Diverse Subjects?" In Y. Taylor (ed.), *Educational Diversity: The Subject of Difference and Different Subjects*. Basingstoke: Palgrave Macmillan, 75–95.

Humanist Society Scotland (undated). "Education without Religion: A Humanist Perspective; Support for Parents and Learners." Accessed online July 12, 2012. http://www.humanism.org.uk/education/teachers/challenging-re

Hughes, M., F. Wikeley, & T. Nash (1994). *Parents and Their Children's Schools*. Oxford: Blackwell.

Hurry, J., L. Rogers, M. Simonot, & A. Wilson (2012). *Inside Education: The Aspirations and Realities of Prison Education for Under 25s in the London Area; A Report for Sir John Cass's Foundation*. London: Institute of Education.

Illich, I. D. (1971). *Deschooling Society*. London: Calder & Boyars Ltd.

The Independent (2013). "Outrage as Failing South Leeds Academy Seeks Unqualified Maths Teachers." Accessed online December 12, 2013. http://www.independent.co.uk/news/education/education-news/

outrage-as-failing-south-leeds-academy-seeks-unqualified-maths-teachers-8957741.html

The Independent (2014). "70 Per Cent of Free Schools Not Filled Two Years after Opening, Labour Claims." April 23. Accessed online April 25, 2014. http://www.independent.co.uk/news/education/schools/70-per-cent-of-free-schools-not-filled-two-years-after-opening-labour-claims-9278569.html

Ingle, S. & V. Duckworth (2013). *Teaching and Training Vocational Learners*. London: Sage and Learning Matters.

Jackson, C. (2003). "Motives for 'Laddishness' at School: Fear of Failure and Fear of the Feminine." *British Educational Research Journal*. 29 (4), 583–98.

Jackson, P. W. (2011). *What Is Education?* Chicago: The University of Chicago Press.

Jonassen, D. H. & S. M. Land (2000). *Theoretical Foundations of Learning Environments*. Mahwah, NJ: Lawrence Erlbaum Associates.

Jones, G. E. & G. W. Roderick (2003). *A History of Education in Wales*. Cardiff: University of Wales Press.

Juvonen, J. & S. Graham (2001). *Peer Harassment in School: The Plight of the Vulnerable and Victimized*. New York: The Guilford Press.

Kalyuga, S., P. Ayres, P. Chandler, & J. Sweller (2003). "The Expertise Reversal Effect." *Educational Psychologist*. 38 (1), 23–31.

Kay, J. (2002). *Teaching Assistant's Handbook*. London: Continuum.

Keating, I. & R. Moorcroft (eds.) (2006). *Managing the Business of Schools*. London: Sage Publications.

Kerr, K. & M. West (2010). *Social Inequality: Can Schools Narrow the Gap?* Macclesfield: British Educational Research Association.

Kinchin, I. M. (2004). "Investigating Students' Beliefs about Their Preferred Role as Learners." *Educational Research*. 46 (3), 301–12.

King, E. C. (2006). "The Roles of Student Musicians in Quartet Rehearsals." *Psychology of Music*. 34 (2), 262–82.

Kinsella, A. & A. Pitman (eds.) (2012). *Professional Knowledge: Practical Wisdom in the Professions*. Rotterdam: Sense.

Korthagen, F. A. J. (in cooperation with J. Kessels et al.) (2001). *Linking Practice and Theory: The Pedagogy of Realistic Teacher Education*. Mahwah, NJ: Lawrence Erlbaum Associates.

Knowles, M. S. (1980). *The Modern Practice of Adult Education*. New York: Cambridge, The Adult Education Company.

Kupfer, J. H. (1990). *Autonomy and Social Interaction*. Albany: University of New York Press.

Laird, J. (1931). "On Doing One's Best." *Philosophy.* 6 (21), 56–71.

Lansdown, G. (2001). *Promoting Children's Participation in Democratic Decision-Making.* Accessed online March 16, 2014. http://www.unicef-irc.org/publications/pdf/insight6.pdf

Laurillard, D. (2002). *Rethinking University Teaching.* London: RoutledgeFalmer.

Learning Wales (2012). "Continuing Professional Development (CPD)." Accessed online April 25, 2014. http://learning.wales.gov.uk/yourcareer/continuingprofessionaldevelopment/?lang=en

Leaton Gray, S. (2006). *Teachers Under Siege.* Stoke-on-Trent: Trentham Books Ltd.

Levin, B. (1998). "An Epidemic of Education Policy: What Can We Learn from Each Other?' *Comparative Education,* 34 (2), 131–41.

Levin, B. (2003). "Approaches to Equity in Policy for Lifelong Learning: A Paper Commissioned by the Education and Training Policy Division, OECD, for the Equity in Education Thematic Review." Accessed online April 11, 2014. http://www.oecd.org/education/innovation-education/38692676.pdf

Lewis, M. (2007). *The Bristol Guide: Professional Responsibilities and Statutory Frameworks for Teachers and Others in Schools.* Bristol: University of Bristol.

Likierman, H. & V. Muter (2006). *Prepare Your Child for School: How to Make Sure Your Child Gets Off to a Flying Start.* London: Vermiliion.

Lines, D. (2008). *The Bullies: Understanding Bullies and Bullying.* London: Jessica Kingsley Publishers.

Lingard, B. & J. Ozga (eds.) (2007). *The RoutledgeFalmer Reader in Education Policy and Politics.* London: Routledge.

Lingfield, R. (2012). *Professionalism in Further Education: Interim Report of the Independent Review Panel.* London: Crown.

Little, B. & R. Williams (2010). "Students' Roles in Maintaining Quality and in Enhancing Learning: Is There a Tension?" *Quality in Higher Education.* 16 (2), 115–27.

Little, D. (1995). "Learning as Dialogue: The Dependence of Learner Autonomy on Teacher Autonomy." *System* 23 (2), 175–81.

Local Government Association (2013). *Higher Education Institutions and Local Government: Collaborating for Growth.* London: Local Government Association.

LSIS (2013). *Teaching and Training Qualifications for the Further Education and Skills Sector in England (2013): Guidance for Employers and Practitioners.* Coventry: Learning and Skills Improvement Service.

Lucas, H. (2011). *After Summerhill*. Bristol: Herbert Adler Publishing.
Lumby, J. (2007). "Parent Voice: Knowledge, Values and Viewpoint." *Improving Schools*. 10 (3), 220–32.
Lumby, J. & N. Foskett (2005). *14–19 Education: Policy, Leadership and Learning*. London: Sage Publications.
Lundy, L. (2007). "Northern Ireland." In J. Russo, D. J. Stewart, & J. De Groof (eds.), *The Educational Rights of Students*. Lanham: Rowman & Littlefield Education, 161–77.
Lundy, L., L. Emerson, K. Lloyd, B. Byrne, & J. Yohanis (2013). *Education Reform in Northern Ireland: A Human Rights Review*. Belfast: Northern Ireland Human Rights Commission.
LV= Travel Insurance (2012). "A 'Fine' Time for a Family Holiday." March. Accessed online July 25, 2012 http://www.lv.com/media_centre/press_releases/fine-time-for-a-family-holiday
Lynch, K. and A. Lodge (2002). *Equality and Power in Schools: Redistribution, Recognition and Representation*. London: Routledgefalmer.
MacBeath, J., M. Galton, S. Steward, A. MacBeath, & C. Page (2006). *The Costs of Inclusion*. Cambridge: University of Cambridge.
MacBeath, J., P. Gronn, D. Opfer, K. Lowden, C. Forde, M. Cowie, & J. O'Brien (2009). *The Recruitment and Retention of Headteachers in Scotland (Main Report)*. Edinburgh: Scottish government.
Machan, T. R. (2000). *Education in a Free Society*. Stanford, CA: Hoover Institution Press.
Machin, S., S. McNally, & G. Wyness (2013). *Education in a Devolved Scotland: A quantitative analysis; Report to the Economic and Social Research Council, March 2013*. Special Paper No. 30. Accessed online August 9, 2013. http://cep.lse.ac.uk/pubs/download/special/cepsp30.pdf
Maer, L. & A. Horne (2009). *Background to Proposals for a British Bill of Rights and Duties*. Standard Note: SN/PC/04559. Accessed online October 28, 2013. www.parliament.uk/briefing-papers/SN04559.pdf
Maloney, J. (2007). "Children's Roles and Use of Evidence in Science: An Analysis of Decision-Making in Small Groups." *British Education Research Journal*. 33 (3), 371–401.
Marble, S., S. Finley, & C. Ferguson (2000). *Understanding Teachers' Perspectives on Teaching and Learning*. Austin: Southwest Educational Development Laboratory.
Markus, H. & P. Nurius (1987). "Possible Selves: The Interface between Motivation and the Self-Concept." In K. Yardley & T. Honess, *Self and Identity: Psychosocial Processes*. Chichester: John Wiley & Sons Ltd., 157–72.

Marshall, J. D. (1996). *Michel Foucault: Personal Autonomy and Education*. Dordrecht: Kluwer Academic Publishers.
McBride, C. (2013). *Recognition*. Cambridge: Polity.
McCourt, F. (2000). *Teacher Man*. London: Fourth Estate.
McGlynn, C. (2004). "Education for Peace in Integrated Schools: A Priority for Northern Ireland?" *Child Care in Practice*. 10 (2), 85–94.
McKenna, K. & L. Day (2010). *Parents' and Young People's Complaints about Schools*. Department for Education Research Report, DFE-RR193.
McKeown, S. (2013). *Identity, Segregation and Peace-Building in Northern Ireland: A Social Psychological Perspective*. Basingstoke: Palgrave Macmillan.
McQueen, H., P. Wilcox, D. Stephen, & C. Walker (2009). *Widening Participation and the Role of Social Motivation in Students' Transitional Experiences in Higher Education*. University of Brighton: SSPARC Report.
McQueen, H. & M. Varvarigou (2010). "Learning through Life." In S. Hallam & A. Creech (eds.), *Music Education in the 21st Century in the United Kingdom: Achievements, Analysis and Aspirations*. London: Bedford Way Papers.
McQueen, H., S. Hallam, A. Creech, & M. Varvarigou (2013). "A Philosophical Perspective on Leading Music Activities for the Over 50s." *International Journal of Lifelong Education*. 32 (3), 353–77.
McQueen, H. & J. Webber (2013). "What Is an Effective Learner? A Comparison of Further Education Students' Views with a Theoretical Construction of Effective Learners." *Journal of Further and Higher Education*. 37 (5): 715–35.
Mehta, S., I. Suto, & S. Brown (2012). *How Effective Are Curricula for 16 to 19 Year Olds as Preparation for University? A Qualitative Investigation of Lecturers' Views*. Cambridge: Cambridge Assessment.
Meyer, B., N. Haywood, D. Sachdev, & S. Faraday (2008). *Independent Learning: Literature Review*. Annesley: DCSF Publications.
Miller, D. (2001). "Distributing Responsibilities." In A. Kuper (ed.) (2005), *Global Responsibilities: Who Must Deliver on Human Rights?* London: Routledge, 95–115.
Mirza, H. S. (2009). *Race, Gender and Educational Desire: Why Black Women Succeed and Fail*. Abingdon: Routledge.
Molesworth, M., E. Nixon, & S. Scullion (2009). "Having, Being and Higher Education: The Marketisation of the University and the Transformation of the Student into Consumer." *Teaching in Higher Education*. 14 (3), 277–87.

Monk, D. (2009). "Parental Responsibility and Education: Taking a Long View." In R. Probert, S. Gilmore, & J. Herring (2009), *Responsible Parents and Parental Responsibility*. Oxford: Hart Publishing, 143–64.

Moon, N. and C. Ivins (2004). "Parental Involvement in Children's Education." DfES research report 589.

Mumsnet (2012). Accessed online July 18, 2012 http://www.mumsnet.com/info/aboutus

Munn, P. & G. Lloyd (2005). "Exclusion and Excluded Pupils." *British Educational Research Journal*. 31 (2), 205–21.

Myhill, D. (2002). "Bad Boys and Good Girls? Patterns of Interaction and Response in Whole Class Teaching." *British Educational Research Journal*. 28 (3), 339–52.

Nordensvärd, J. (2011). "The Consumer Metaphor versus the Citizen Metaphor: Different Sets of Roles for Students." In M. Molesworth, R. Scullion, & E. Nixon (eds.), *The Marketisation of Higher Education and the Student as Consumer*. Abingdon, Routledge 157–169.

Northern Ireland Assembly (2013). "Minutes of Proceedings: Wednesday 11 September 2013." Accessed online January 16, 2014. http://www.niassembly.gov.uk/Documents/Education/minutes/20130911.pdf

Northern Ireland Curriculum. Accessed online August 9, 2013. http://www.nicurriculum.org.uk/about/

Northern Ireland Curriculum (2007). *Personal Development and Mutual Understanding for Key Stages 1 & 2*. Belfast: The Partnership Management Board.

Northern Ireland Executive (2011). *Programme for Government 2011–15*. Accessed online September 27, 2013. http://www.northernireland.gov.uk/

Northern Ireland Executive Strategy (2011). "Economic Strategy." Belfast: NI Economic Strategy Consultation.

Norwich, B. (2013). *Addressing Tensions and Dilemmas in Inclusive Education: Living with Uncertainty*. Abingdon: Routledge.

NSPCC (National Society for the Prevention of Cruelty to Children) (2013) "Safeguarding in Education Service: Briefing; The Role of the Designated Senior Person (DSP) for Child Protection in Schools and Colleges." Accessed online December 31, 2013. http://www.nspcc.org.uk/Inform/resourcesforteachers/designated-sr-person/roleofdsp-briefing_wdf88593.pdf

NUS (National Union of Students) (2008). "Think about Becoming a Course Rep." Accessed online February 19, 2014. http://www.nus.org.uk/cy/advice/course-reps/think-about-becoming-a-course-rep/

NUT (National Union of Teachers) Notes 2012–13. Accessed online August 16, 2013. http://www.teachers.org.uk/files/the-law-and-you--8251-.pdf

OECD (2012). *Equity and Quality in Education: Supporting Disadvantaged Students and Schools.* OECD (Organisation for Economic Co-operation and Development) Publishing. http://dx.doi.org/10.1787/9789264130852-en

Office for National Statistics (2012). *Ethnicity and National Identity in England and Wales (2011).* London: Crown.

Ofqual (2013). *Statistical Bulletin: Appeals for GCSE and A level: Summer 2012 Exam Series.* Coventry: Office of Qualifications and Examinations Regulation.

Ofsted (2007). "Stoke Hill Infant and Nursery School: Inspection Report." Accessed online February 19, 2014. http://www.ofsted.gov.uk/filedownloading/?id=955265&type=1&refer=1

Ofsted (2011). "Summerhill School: Inspection report." London: Crown.

Oancea, A. & J. Orchard (2012). "The Future of Teacher Education." In R. Smith (ed.) (2013), *Education Policy: Philosophical Critique.* Chichester: Wiley Blackwell, 74–88.

Orfield, G. & E. Frankenberg (2013). *Educational Delusions? Why Choice Can Deepen Inequality and How to Make Schools Fair.* Berkeley, CA: University of California Press.

Oshana, M. (2006). *Personal Autonomy in Society.* Aldershot: Ashgate Publishing Ltd.

Osler, J. & J. Flack (2008). *Whose Learning Is It? Developing Children as Active and Responsible Learners.* Rotterdam: Sense Publishers.

Oxford Learning Institute (2012). "Tutorial Teaching." Accessed online December 28, 2013. http://www.learning.ox.ac.uk/support/teaching/resources/teaching/

Paradice, R. and A. Adewusi (2002). "It's a Continuous Fight Isn't It? Parents' Views on the Educational Provision for Children with Speech and Language Difficulties." *Child Language Teaching and Therapy.* 18 (2), 257–88.

Parent.org (2014). Accessed online April 11, 2014. http://www.parenting.org/article/responsibility-part-ii

Parent View (online survey). Department for Education. Accessed online July 12, 2012 http://www.education.gov.uk/schools/pupilsupport/parents/involvement/a00200782/parent-view

Parents Outloud. Accessed online January 16, 2014. http://www.parentsoutloud.com/about/

Parish, N., A. Baxter, & L. Sandals (2012). *Action Research into the Evolving Role of the Local Authority in Education: The Final Report for the Ministerial Advisory Group.* ISOS Partnership. DFE-RR224. Accessed online October 28, 2013. https://www.gov.uk/government/uploads/system/uploads/attachment_data/file/184055/DFE-RR224.pdf

Parry, G., C. Callender, P. Scott, & P. Temple (2012). "Understanding Higher Education in Further Education Colleges." Research paper 69. London: Department for Business, Innovation and Skills.

Paterson, L. (2013). "Comprehensive Education, Social Attitudes and Civic Engagement." *Longitudinal and Life Course Studies.* 4 (1), 17–32.

Peczenik, A. & M. M. Karlsson (eds.) (1995). *Law, Justice and the State I: Essays on Justice and Rights.* Stuttgart: Franz Steiner Verlag.

Phillips, D. (2000). *The Education Systems of the United Kingdom.* Oxford: Symposium Books.

Piaget, J. (1936). *La Naissance de l'Intelligence chez l'Enfant.* Neuchatel: Delachaux et Niestlé.

Plaid Cymru (2013). "Welsh Government Response to Hill Education Review 'Damp Squib.'" October 25, 2013. Accessed online November 1, 2013. http://www.english.simonthomas.plaidcymru.org/news/2013/10/25/welsh-government-response-to-hill-education-review-damp-squib/

Powell, J. (1996). "Professional and Client." In P. Birks (ed.), *Wrongs and Remedies in the Twenty-First Century.* Oxford: Clarendon Press, 47–66.

Power, S. & D. Frandji (2010). "Education Markets, the New Politics of Recognition and the Increasing Fatalism towards Inequality." *Journal of Education Policy.* 25 (3), 385–96.

Pritchard, A. & J. Woollard (2010). *Psychology for the Classroom: Constructivism and Social Learning.* London: Routledge.

Puffin Books online. Accessed online July 18, 2012. http://www.puffin.co.uk/nf/Book/BookDisplay/0,,9780140507379,00.html

QAA (2008). "The Framework for Higher Education Qualifications in England, Wales and Northern Ireland." Mansfield: Quality Assurance Agency for Higher Education.

"QCA Coursework: A Guide for Parents." Accessed online July 18, 2012. www.qca.org.uk/courseworkleaflet

REF (2012). Accessed online January 4, 2014. http://www.ref.ac.uk/

Rauscher, F. H., G. L. Shaw, & K. N. Ky (1995). "Listening to Mozart Enhances Spatial Temporal Reasoning: Towards a Neurophysiological Basis." *Neuroscience Letters.* 195, 44–47.

Riddell, S., E. Weedon, L. Ahlgren, & G. McCluskey (2009). *Religious Education in a Multi-Cultural Society: Scotland National Report.* Edinburgh: European Union.

RISE (Research and Information on State Education) (2004). *Parent Governor Representatives—A Bigger Say for Parents?* Keele University. Accessed online July 23, 2012. http://risetrust.org.uk/pdfs/pgr2004.pdf

Robson, J. (1998). "A Profession in Crisis: Status, Culture and Identity in the Further Education College." *Journal of Vocational Education and Training.* 50 (4), 585–607.

Rogers, C. R. (1983). *Freedom to Learn for the 80s.* New York: Macmillan.

Rothermel, P. (2003). "Can We Classify Motives for Home Education?" *Research in Education* 17 (2–3), 74–89.

Rouse, M. & L. Florian (2012). *Inclusive Practice Project: Final Report.* Accessed online January 4, 2013. http://www.academia.edu/4432038/The_Inclusive_Practice_Project_Final_Report

Rousseau, J. J. (1979 [1762]) *Emile or On Education.* Trans. A. Bloom. New York: Basic Books.

Rudduck, J. & J. Flutter (2000). "Pupil Participation and Pupil Perspective: 'Carving a New Order of Experience.'" *Cambridge Journal of Education.* 30 (1), 75–89.

Russell Group (2013). Accessed online January 4, 2014. http://www.russellgroup.ac.uk/home/

Ryan, K. & J. M. Cooper (2007). *Those Who Can, Teach.* 12th edition. Boston, MA: Wadsworth Cengage Learning.

Ryan, M. R. & E. L. Deci (2001). "On Happiness and Human Potentials: A Review of Research on Hedonic and Eudaimonic Well-Being." *Annual Review of Psychology.* 52, 141–66.

Sahlberg, P. (2011). *Finnish Lessons: What Can the World Learn from Educational Change in Finland?* New York: Teachers College Press.

Salmivalli, C. (1999). "Participant Role Approach to School Bullying: Implications for Interventions." *Journal of Adolescence.* 22 (4), 453–9.

School Boards (Scotland) Act (1988). London: HMSO.

School Standards and Framework Act (1998). Accessed online July 23, 2012. http://www.legislation.gov.uk/ukpga/1998/31/contents/enacted

Scottish Executive (2006a). "Positive about Pupil Participation." Edinburgh: Crown.

Scottish Executive (2006b). "Scottish Schools (Parental Involvement) Act 2006: Guidance." Edinburgh: Crown.

Scottish government (2007). "Annex D: Recommendations on Staffing, Learners and Learning Environments." Accessed online December 31, 2013. http://www.scotland.gov.uk/Publications/2007/06/27151710/8

Scottish government (2010). "Curriculum for Excellence: Building the Curriculum 2—Active Learning, a Guide to Developing Professional Practice." Glasgow: Crown.

Scottish government (2011). Accessed online November 8, 2013. http://www.scotland.gov.uk/Topics/Education/Schools/FAQs

Scottish government (2013). "Health and Wellbeing in Curriculum for Excellence." Accessed online January 3, 2014. http://www.scotland.gov.uk/Topics/Education/Schools/HLivi

Sennett, R. (2008). *The Craftsman*. London: Allen Lane and Penguin.

Sherbert Research (2009). *Parents as Partners: "Harder to Engage" Parents*. Nottingham: Department for Children, Schools and Families (now the Department for Education). Research Report DCSF-RR111.

Shier, H. (2001). "Pathways to Participation: Openings, Opportunities and Obligations." *Children and Society*. 15, 101–117.

SNCT (Scottish Negotiating Committee for Teachers) (2001). "A Teaching Profession for the 21st Century." Accessed online December 18, 2013. http://www.snct.org.uk/library/278/2001%20Teachers%20Agreement.pdf

SNCT (2007). *SNCT Handbook*. Accessed online December 29, 2013. http://www.snct.org.uk/

Solomon, Y., J. Warin, & C. Lewis (2002). "Helping with Homework? Homework as a Site of Tension for Parents and Teenagers." *British Educational Research Journal*. 28 (4), 603–22.

sparqs. Accessed online November 12, 2013. http://www.sparqs.ac.uk/

Spielhofer, S., M. Walker, K. Gagg, S. Schagen, & S. O'Donnell (2007). *Raising the Participation Age in Education and Training to 18: Review of Existing Evidence of the Benefits and Challenges*. National Foundation for Educational Research. Research Report DCSF-RR012. Annesley: DfES Publications.

Steer, A. (2009). "Learning Behaviour: Lessons Learner; A Review of Behaviour Standards and Practices in Our Schools." Nottingham: DCSF Publications.

Steinberg, L., S. D. Lamborn, S. M. Dornbusch, & N. Darling (1992). "Impact of Parenting Practices on Adolescent Achievement: Authoritative Parenting, School Involvement, and Encouragement to Succeed." *Child Development*. 63, 1266–81.

Stevenson, J. & S. Clegg (2011). "Possible Selves: Students Orientating Themselves towards the Future through Extracurricular Activity." *British Educational Research Journal*. 37 (2), 231–46.

Stewart, D. J., C. J. Russo, & J. De Groof (2007). "Introduction." In J. Russo, D. J. Stewart, & J. De Groof (eds.), *The Educational Rights of Students*. Lanham: Rowman & Littlefield Education, 1–7.

Stobart, G. (2014). *The Expert Learner: Challenging the Myth of Ability.* Maidenhead: Open University Press.

Stojanov, K. (2010). "Overcoming Social Pathologies in Education: On the Concept of Respect in R. S. Peters and Axel Honneth." *Journal of Philosophy of Education.* 43 (1), 161–72.

Summerhill website. Accessed online March 13 2014. http://www.summerhillschool.co.uk/summerhills-fight.php

"Summerhill: The Early Days" (2004). Summerhill. Accessed online August 12, 2013 http://www.summerhillschool.co.uk/pages/history.html

Super, C. and S. Harkness (1986). "The Developmental Niche: A Conceptualisation at the Interface of Child and Culture." *International Journal of Behavioural Development.* 9, 545–69.

The Sutton Trust (2011). *What Prospects for Mobility in the UK? A Cross-National Study of Educational Inequalities and Their Implications for Future Education and Earnings Mobility.* Accessed online January 15, 2014. http://www.suttontrust.com/public/documents/1sutton-trust-crita-summary-23-11-11.pdf

Swann, S. (2013). *Pupil Disaffection in Schools: Bad Boys and Hard Girls.* Farnham: Ashgate.

Tarleton, B., L. Ward, & J. Howarth (2006). *Finding the Right Support? A Review of Issues and Positive Practice in Supporting Parents with Learning Difficulties and Their Children.* London: The Baring Foundation.

Taverner, D. (1994). "The Changing Roles and Responsibilities of School Governance." In W. Tulasiewicz & G. Strowbridge (eds.) (1994), *Education and the Law: International Perspectives.* London: Routledge, 199–210.

Taylor, C. (1994). "The Politics of Recognition." In A. Gutmann (ed.), *Multiculturalism: Examining the Politics of Recognition.* New Jersey: Princeton University Press, 5–75.

Taylor, C. (2011). *Getting the Simple Things Right: Charlie Taylor's Behaviour Checklists.* Accessed online September 19, 2013. https://www.gov.uk/government/uploads/system/uploads/attachment_data/file/283997/charlie_taylor_checklist.pdf

Teachers' Pay and Conditions of Service Inquiry: Final Report—Part 2; Improving Conditions, Raising Standards and Negotiating Arrangements

(2004). Accessed online December 29, 2013. http://www.atl.org.uk/Images/NI%20pay%20and%20conditions%20final%20report%202.pdf

The Telegraph (2001). "Euan Blair Is Made Deputy Head Boy." Accessed online January 30, 2014. http://www.telegraph.co.uk/news/uknews/1309459/Euan-Blair-is-made-deputy-head-boy.html

The Telegraph (2002). "Tearaway Becomes Top of the Class." Accessed online January 30, 2014. http://www.telegraph.co.uk/news/uknews/3302901/Tearaway-becomes-top-of-the-class.html

The Telegraph (2009). "Ofsted Is a Government Poodle, Say MPs." July 8. Accessed online September 26, 2013. http://www.telegraph.co.uk/education/educationnews/5779610/Ofsted-is-a-Government-poodle-say-MPs.html

The Telegraph (2010). "David Cameron Calls for More Faith Schools." January 26. Accessed online November 8, 2013. http://www.telegraph.co.uk/education/educationnews/7073322/David-Cameron-calls-for-more-faith-schools.html

The Telegraph (August 12, 2013). Accessed online August 12, 2013. http://www.telegraph.co.uk/education/educationnews/10236432/Universities-reject-Michael-Goves-A-level-plan.html

Thomson, B., G. Mawdsley, & A. Payne (2009). *Parent Power*. Accessed online August 13, 2013. http://reformscotland.com/include/publications/parent_power.pdf

Times Educational Supplement leaked letters (2012). Accessed online October 29, 2013. http://www.tes.co.uk/tesassets/images/resources/Ofqual_Edexcel_Documents_2012.pdf

TES (*Times Educational Supplement*) (2010). "TES Survey—Who's Earning What in Education." Accessed online January 6, 2014. http://www.tes.co.uk/article.aspx?storycode=6039350

TES (2013). "Teaching Assistant Pay and Conditions." Accessed online December 19, 2013. http://www.tes.co.uk/article.aspx?storyCode=6168765

THE (2013). "Gender Survey of UK Professoriate, 2013." Accessed online January 6, 2014. http://www.timeshighereducation.co.uk/news/gender-survey-of-uk-professoriate-2013/2004766.article

Tilstone, C., L. Florian, & R. Rose (eds.) (1998). *Promoting Inclusive Practice*. Abingdon: Routledge.

Tomlinson, M. (2004). *14-19 Curriculum and Qualifications Reform: Final Report of the Working Group on 14-19 Reform*. Annesley: DfES Publications.

Tomlinson, S. (2001). *Education in a Post-Welfare Society*. Buckingham: Open University Press.

Topping, K .J. (2005). "Trends in Peer Learning." *Educational Psychology*. 25 (6), 631–45.

Tyler, T. M. & J. Fagan (2008). "Legitimacy and Cooperation: Why Do People Help the Police Fight Crime in Their Communities?" *Journal of Criminal Law*. 231–75.

Tyler, W. (2012 [1977]). *The Sociology of Educational Inequality*. Abingdon: Routledge.

Tytherleigh, M. Y., C. Webb, C. L. Cooper, & C. Ricketts (2005). "Occupational Stress in UK Higher Education Institutions: A Comparative Study of All Staff Categories." *Higher Education Research and Development*. 24 (1), 41–61.

UCU (University and College Union) website. Accessed online December 30, 2013. http://www.ucu.org.uk/payandconditions

UCU (2012). "The Position of Women and BME Staff in Professorial Roles in UK HEIs." London: UCU.

UNICEF website. "UN Convention on the Rights of the Child." Accessed online March 7, 2014. http://www.unicef.org.uk/UNICEFs-Work/Our-mission/UN-Convention/

UNICEF (1989). "The United Nations Convention on the Rights of the Child." London: UNICEF UK.

United Nations (1948). *Universal Declaration of Human Rights*. 60th anniversary special edition. Accessed online March 13, 2014. http://www.ohchr.org/EN/UDHR/Documents/60UDHR/bookleten.pdf

United Nations (UN). *The Universal Declaration of Human Rights* (1950). Accessed online December 30, 2013. http://www.un.org/en/documents/udhr/index.shtml#a26

United Nations website. "UN at a glance." Accessed online March 7, 2014. http://www.un.org/en/aboutun/index.shtml

University of Bristol (2003). "ELLI—A New Way of Learning." Accessed online February 20, 2014. http://www.bristol.ac.uk/news/2003/190.html

Updike, J. (1959). "Home." In *Pigeon Feathers and Other Stories*. New York: Random House.

Vincent, C. (2012). "Parenting: Responsibilities, Risks and Respect." Professorial Lecture Series. London: Institute of Education.

Vincent, C., N. Rollock, S. Ball, & D. Gillborn (2012). "The Education Strategies of the Black Middle Classes." In M. Richter & S. Andresen (eds.), *The Politicization of Parenthood: Shifting Private and Public*

Responsibilities in Education and Child Rearing. London: Springer, 139–52.

Waldegrave, H. & J. Simons (2014). *Watching the Watchmen: The future of school inspections in England.* London: Policy Exchange.

Wallace, S. (2007). *Getting the Buggers Motivated in FE.* London: Continuum International Publishing Group.

Ward, S. and C. Eden (2009). *Key Issues in Education Policy.* London: Sage.

Watkins, C., E. Carnell, & C. Lodge (2007). *Effective Learning in Classrooms.* London: Paul Chapman Publishing.

Webster, R. & P. Blatchford. "Supporting Learning? How Effective Are Teaching Assistants?" In P. Adey & J. Dillon (eds.), *Debunking Myths in Education.* Maidenhead: Open University Press, 77–91.

Welsh government (2007). "The School Curriculum for Wales." Accessed online August 9, 2013 http://wales.gov.uk/topics/educationandskills/schoolshome/curriculuminwales/arevisedcurriculumforwales/?lang=en

Welsh government (2010). "Welsh-Medium Education Strategy." Accessed online September 27, 2013. http://wales.gov.uk/docs/dcells/publications/100420welshmediumstrategyen.pdf

Welsh government (2011a). "Programme: Education." Accessed online September 26, 2013. http://wales.gov.uk/about/programmeforgov/education/?lang=en

Welsh government (2011b). "Pupil Participation—Good Practice Guide." Crown.

Welsh government (2013). "Wales as It Stands—What Are the Inequalities We Want to Tackle?" Accessed online November 17, 2013. http://wales.gov.uk/topics/equality/publications/5503306/?lang=en

West, A. (1994). "Choosing Schools—The Consumers' Perspective." In M. J. Halstead (ed.), *Parental Choice and Education: Principles, Policy and Practice.* London: Kogan Page Ltd, 108–23.

Westminster Faith Debates (2013). "YouGov Survey Press Release." Accessed online November 9, 2013. http://faithdebates.org.uk/research/

White, A. (2008). *From Comfort Zone to Performance Management: Understanding Development and Performance.* Accessed online March 14, 2014. http://www.whiteandmaclean.eu/uploaded_files/12012010 9110852performance_management-final290110(2)-preview.pdf

Whitebread, D., H. Anderson, P. Coltman, C. Page, D. P. Pasternak, & S. Mehta (2005). "Developing Independent Learning in the Early Years." *Education 3–13: International Journal of Primary, Elementary and Early Years Education.* 33 (1), 40–50.

Whitty, G. & S. Power (2000). "Marketization and Privatization in Mass Education Systems." *International Journal of Educational Development*. 20, 93–107.

Wiliam, D. (2011). *Embedded Formative Assessment*. Bloomington, IN: Solution Tree

Wiliam, D. (2012). "Are There 'Good' Schools and 'Bad' Schools?" In P. Adey & J. Dillon (eds.), *Debunking Myths in Education*. Maidenhead: Open University Press, 3–15.

Wilkinson, H. (2001). "The Family Way: Navigating a Third Way in Family Policy." In A. Giddens (ed.), *The Global Third Way Debate*. Cambridge: Polity Press, 224–32

Wilkinson, R. & K. Pickett (2009). *The Spirit Level: Why Greater Equality Makes Societies Stronger*. New York: Bloomsbury Press.

Wilshaw, M. (2014). Letter to secretary of state (advice note). Accessed online June 13, 2014. http://www.ofsted.gov.uk/resources/advice-note-provided-academies-and-maintained-schools-birmingham-secretary-of-state-for-education-rt

Winch, C. (1999). "Autonomy as an Educational Aim." In R. Marples (ed.), *The Aims of Education*. London: Routledge, 74–83.

Wolf, A. (2002). *Does Education Matter? Myths about Education and Economic Growth*. London: Penguin.

Wolf, A. (2011). *Review of Vocational Education: The Wolf Report*. Accessed online September 27, 2013. https://www.gov.uk/government/publications/review-of-vocational-education-the-wolf-report

Wolfenden, J. F. (1952). "Three Duties of a Teacher." Arthur Mellows Memorial Lecture. September 30 (no publisher cited).

Woodhead, M. (1999). "Reconstructing Developmental Psychology: Some First Steps." *Children & Society*. 13 (1), 1–17.

Woods, P. A. (2011). *Transforming Education Policy: Shaping a Democratic Future*. Bristol: Policy Press.

Wootton, M. (2000). *Duties and Responsibilities*. 4th edition. Upminster: Nightingale Teaching Consultancy.

Wößmann, L. & G. Schütz (2006). "Efficiency and Equity in European Education and Training Systems." Analytical Report for the European Commission prepared by the European Expert Network on Economics of Education (EENEE) to accompany the Communication and Staff Working Paper by the European Commission under the same title. Accessed online November 17, 2013. http://ec.europa.eu/education/policies/2010/doc/eenee.pdf

Wright, C., D. Weekes, & A. McLaughlin (2000). *'Race', Class and Gender in Exclusion from School*. London: Falmer Press.

Index

academic, *see* curriculum; learners' roles
accountability, 28, 33–4, 40, 87, 107, 120, 123, 125, 131, 137–44
autonomy, 19, 34, 40, 56–7, 68, 96–7, 106, 134, 137, 141–5

choice, 2, 24, 34, 37–40, 61, 68, 75, 81, 84–5, 91–3, 96, 97, 98–100, 137–43, 145, 148
  see also consumerism; curriculum; free schools
consumerism, 11, 71, 84, 103
curriculum
  academic-vocational, 10–1, 60–1, 75, 135, 145–9
  education for mutual understanding (EMU) 8, 39, 139
  hidden, 11, 154
  national curriculum, 7, 8, 24, 56, 87, 124

economy, 1, 20–2, 27, 42, 117, 145
  see also consumerism
education
  definition of, 8–11
  home, 84–5, 91, 93

policy, 17–9, 20–1, 23, 32–7, 39, 79, 139, 151, 153
prison, 72, 74
private (fee paid), 2, 84, 93, 142
equality, 80, 88, 91
  and special educational needs, 92
  see also, inequality, rights
equity, 40–1, 127, 149–51
  and choice, 97, 98, 142
  see also inequality

free
  market, 12, 17–8, 142
  schools, 13, 19, 33, 37, 38, 43, 88, 91, 109, 121–2
  society, 65, 138–42
freedom, 48–9, 64, 71, 94–5, 123, 139–40, 143–4

governors, 28–9, 35
  role of, 28, 90, 152
  parent governors, 90, 102

habitus, 57, 60–1, 75, 100, 132
Her Majesty's Inspectorate, *see* quality assurance

home school agreements, 87–8, 97–8
  see also tensions
home schooling, see education, home

inclusion, 92–3, 96, 98, 126–7, 150
  see also tensions
inequality, 39, 40, 41–4, 63–4, 112, 121, 128–30
  and equity, 149–52
  of access and participation, 72–4
  of choice, 75, 98
  of experience, 10–1
  and recognition, 43, 135–6
  socioeconomic, 42, 98
  structural, 13, 37, 44, 76
  see also equality; equity

learner autonomy
learners, 50
  effective, 53, 56–7, 100–1
  see also learners' roles; responsibility of; rights of; role of
learners' roles
  academic-vocational, 60–1
  autonomous-dependent, 56–7
  active-passive, 52
  bully-victim, 62–3
  compliant-resistant, 58–9
  expert-novice, 59–60
  learner-teacher, 60
  past-future, 61–2
local authorities, see role of local governance

parents, 2, 11–13, 28, 37, 79–81, 111, 148
  parental involvement, 81–2, 88–90, 96, 100–1
  see also choice; responsibility of; rights of; role of; stakeholders
policy, see education policy
prison education, see education
private education, see education
professionalism, 12, 25, 34, 105–7

quality assurance, 20, 23–5, 26, 28, 35, 39, 65

recognition, 43, 133–6
responsibility, 3, 12–4
  meaning of, 13–4, 126, 137–8
responsibility of
  governance, 33–6, 44
  learners, 49, 52, 56, 67–8, 73, 144
  parents, 80, 81, 83, 85, 88, 91, 94–6, 99
  teachers, 111–2, 120–1, 125–6, 127
rights, 4, 139
rights of
  governance, 32–3
  learners, 47, 52, 63–7, 72–3
  parents, 89, 91–3, 94, 96
  teachers, 12, 118–9
role of
  central government and agencies, 18, 22–6
  Her Majesty's Inspectorate, 25
  learners, 47, 50–1, 52–63, 67, 144

local governance and
  management, 26–32, 39
parents, 12, 83–90, 100–1,
  102, 103
stakeholders, 31–2
teachers, 13, 60, 69, 107, 108,
  109–18, 120, 138, 141, 143
teaching assistants, 127, 130

senior management, 1, 29–31
special educational needs, *see*
  rights of learners; inequality
stakeholders, 17, 27, 34, 63, 153
see also role of stakeholders

teachers, *see* responsibility of;
  rights of; role of;
teaching assistants (TA), *see*
  responsibility of; role of
teaching methods, 10, 49, 54–5,
  65, 67, 70–1, 85, 96, 108,
  109, 115, 123, 126, 139,
  141, 150
tensions
  autonomy-dependence, 68–9
  choice-equity, 97
  consumerism in education, 71

diversity and social
  cohesion, 152
emotional well-being and
  achievement, 124–5
equity and efficiency, 40–1
home-school agreements, 97
inclusion, 126–7
learner comfort or risk and
  challenge, 69–71
neoliberalism, choice and social
  unity, 37–40
practical-theoretical, 108–9,
  122–3
qualified-unqualified teachers,
  121–2
and recognition, 135
responsibility, accountability
  and blame, 125–6, 138
teaching and research in higher
  education, 127–8

United Kingdom, 6–8, 15, 18,
  19–22, 23–28, 31, 32,
  36–40, 41, 43–4, 63–4, 152

vocational, *see* curriculum;
  habitus; learners' roles

GPSR Compliance

The European Union's (EU) General Product Safety Regulation (GPSR) is a set of rules that requires consumer products to be safe and our obligations to ensure this.

If you have any concerns about our products, you can contact us on

ProductSafety@springernature.com

In case Publisher is established outside the EU, the EU authorized representative is:

Springer Nature Customer Service Center GmbH
Europaplatz 3
69115 Heidelberg, Germany

www.ingramcontent.com/pod-product-compliance
Lightning Source LLC
LaVergne TN
LVHW012101070526
838200LV00074BA/3890